# CHARACTERS

**Fairy Thistledown**
**Alonzo**, the Court Chamberlain
**Dame Goodheart**, the Royal Housekeeper
**Voice of the Spirit of the Mirror**
**Queen Maligna**, Ruler of Sylvania
**Chuckles**, the Court Jester
**Princess Millie**, known as **Snow White**
**Prince Michael of Tyrolia**

**Campion**
**Mouse-ear**
**Sorrel**
**Cloudberry** } The Seven Friends
**Butterburr**
**Coltsfoot**
**Speedwell**

Chorus of **Citizens, Courtiers, Fairies, Spirits**, etc.

## COPYRIGHT INFORMATION

(See also page ii)

# Snow White

A pantomime

## Norman Robbins

## Samuel French — London

New York - Toronto - Hollywood

# SYNOPSIS OF THE SCENES

**ACT I**

**INTERVAL**

**ACT II**

## AUTHOR'S NOTE

There can be few people in Britain who have not been enthralled by Walt Disney's 1937 animated film classic of *Snow White* and, perhaps because of this, other adapters of the story have had to tread warily through the dangerous minefields of copyright. The Disney version is so entrenched in our collective minds, that audiences expect to see exactly the same show on the stage, and are sometimes most upset when they don't get it. Both music and names of most characters, for instance, were copyrighted by the Disney Organization, and no-one else can use them. Likewise, the animated antics are impossible to recreate convincingly on stage, but audiences, not appreciating this, often feel cheated when they don't see them. So why do we writers bother? The answer is simple. It's a wonderful story and as interesting today as when the Grimm brothers presented it to the world in 1819.

In response to many requests over the years, I have written this version in pantomime form. It has a fairy (who plays the role of Narrator), a "Dame", a "Simple Simon" character, and a Principal Boy who appears in a lot of Act I instead of just a fleeting appearance at the end of Act II. Music I leave to the Director's choice, though I have prepared a list of suggested songs, totally unconnected to the Disney version, which is available from me c/o Samuel French Ltd. Just keep the pace brisk, treat it as a true pantomime, and I'm sure your audiences will respond with enthusiasm.

Norman Robbins

For
Karen and John Watkins
(a small appreciation for kindness and company)

## MUSIC

A list of song suggestions is available from the author c/o Samuel French Ltd.

A licence issued by Samuel French Ltd to perform this play does not include permission to use the music specified in this copy. Where the place of performance is already licensed by the PERFORMING RIGHT SOCIETY a return of the music used must be made to them. If the place of performance is not so licensed then application should be made to the Performing Right Society, 29 Berners Street, London W1.

A separate and additional licence from PHONOGRAPHIC PERFORMANCES LTD, Ganton House, Ganton Street, London W1 is needed whenever commercial recordings are used.

Other pantomimes by Norman Robbins
published by Samuel French Ltd

Aladdin
Ali Baba and the Forty Thieves
Babes in the Wood
Cinderella
Dick Whittington
The Grand Old Duke of York
Hickory Dickory Dock
Humpty Dumpty
Jack and the Beanstalk
Puss in Boots
Rumpelstiltskin
Sing a Song of Sixpence
The Sleeping Beauty
Tom, the Piper's Son
The Wonderful Story of Mother Goose


Full-length plays by Norman Robbins
published by Samuel French Ltd

The Late Mrs Early
Nightmare
Pull the Other One
Slaughterhouse
A Tomb with a View
Wedding of the Year

# ACT I

*The Land of Fairy Tale*

*The* CURTAIN *rises on a dark lanecloth*

*The Fairy enters* R, *in a white follow spot*

**Fairy**     Thrice welcome, gentle mortals, to the land of Fairy Tale;
       Where dreams come true, and 'gainst all evil,
       Goodness ever will prevail.
       So settle back and listen to our story for tonight,
       A tale of mirth and mystery: The legend of "Snow White".

*She strikes a story-telling attitude*

  (*With feeling*) In ancient times, a king and queen
       In bliss, reigned o'er their kingdom wide,
       But, sad to say, upon the day
       Their child was born, the poor queen died.
       In grief, the king shed bitter tears,
       His heart was filled with pain;
       Though he loved his daughter, still he vowed,
       He'd never, ever, smile again.
       And yet, at last, his heartache passed;
       His eyes he mopped and dried.
       To give his child a mother,
       Once again he took a bride.
       Her beauty quite exceptional,
       Ensnared him in a trice,
       But little did the good king know,
       Her wicked heart was cold as ice.
       With poison in his chalice
       She then claimed the royal throne
       And at her mercy, young Snow White

Was left, alas, alone.
(*Brightly*)        Now join us in Sylvania,
Where the characters await
To show you all what happens next ...
And how the princess met her fate.


SCENE 1

*The City Square in Sylvania. Day*

*A typical pantomime setting of half-timbered houses and shops against a backdrop of thick forest. Buildings* UR *and* UL, *hide exits and entrances. One of these buildings is an antique shop with a practical door*

*When the Lights come up, it is a sunny day, and the Citizens in bright, medieval costumes are singing and dancing happily*

**No. 1** Song (Citizens)

*At the end of the song, all gather into small groups, laughing and chattering*

*Alonzo, the Court Chamberlain hurries on* UL *and moves* C. *He is a fussy and elderly personage who exists in a constant state of anxiety*

**Alonzo** (*urgently*) What's happening? What's going on? Why is everyone singing and dancing in the streets? We can hear you in the royal palace. (*He indicates off* L)
**Citizens** (*brightly*) Good-morning, Lord Chamberlain.
**Alonzo** (*wincing*) Not so *loud*. If you wake her majesty, we'll *all* be in trouble. (*He casts a worried look off* L)
**Girl** I don't see why. We're only doing what we were told to do.
**Man** Yes. We've to celebrate from dawn to sunset or suffer the consequences. The messenger said so. It's the queen's own command.
**Alonzo** (*surprised*) Is it? (*Upset*) Oh dear, I don't know *what's* got into her lately. She's acting more strangely than ever. (*He glances around to make sure he is not being overheard*) Last night, she was so angry, she sent the palace guards down to the station and told them to *cross the railway lines.* (*Wearily*) It's taken us *hours* to straighten them out again. (*He sighs*)
**Man** (*kindly*) Never mind, Lord Chamberlain. At least she'll feel happier today. Once the guests start arriving and the party begins, she'll ——
**Alonzo** (*startled*) Party? (*He glances around*) *What* party?

*Everyone looks puzzled*

**Girl** (*surprised*) Why, her *birthday* party, of course.
**Alonzo** (*baffled*) Birthday party? (*He gives a little laugh and shakes his head*) I'm afraid there's some mistake. It won't be her birthday for *ages*. I've got the date right here in my Fourteenth-Century Filofax. Look. (*He fumbles in his robe and produces a large calendar which he consults*) Queen Maligna's Birthday. Friday. The thirteenth of … Oh. (*Aghast*) Oh no. It *is* today. It *is*. (*Stricken*) What am I going to do? I haven't sent a card or even bought her a present. (*He groans*) She'll be furious. Absolutely *furious*. (*He presses his nails into his mouth*)
**Man** No, she won't. You've still got time. Pop into the antique shop over there (*he indicates*) and find her something unusual. You know how she loves curiosities. (*Sourly*) Especially expensive ones.

*All agree ruefully*

**Alonzo** (*relieved*) You're right. Of course. Oh, I don't know how to thank you. I'll do it at once. This very minute. Immediately. Now.

*He hurries off into the shop*

**Girl** (*to the others with a sigh*) And we'd better finish buying our presents, too, if we don't want her getting annoyed with *us*.

*All exit morosely. As they do so, Dame Goodheart enters* UR *and moves* C. *She is a lady of very uncertain age, and is the Royal Housekeeper. She carries a shopping bag*

**Dame** (*seeing the audience*) Oh, I say. I'd forgotten we had tourists in tonight. But of course we have, haven't we? (*She beams at them*) Well, it *is* nice to see you. We like a few visitors now and then. You feel ever so daft up here if nobody's watching. (*She laughs*) Mind you, we get people from all over the place, you know. Oh, yes. In fact, there's a very big party in from (*local area*) tonight. Here she is — sitting in the second row. (*She chortles*) Oooh, I do like to see a big woman laughing. So much of her has a good time. (*She chortles*) Anyway, it's nice to see you all, and before we go any further, I'd better introduce myself, hadn't I? Goodheart's the name. Dame Goodheart. Royal Housekeeper, and widow of this parish. (*She simpers*) Oh, yes. I'm very well known about here, you know. Well, I do a lot of what they call "Good works". Sort of — visiting the poorly people and cheering them up. (*She winces*) Ooh, and aren't there some poorly people around these days? There's one feller in (*local street*) that thinks he's a pair of curtains. (*She sniffs*) I told him to pull himself together. (*As the thought strikes her*) Here, and aren't the "Get Well" cards expensive? (*She gets one out of her bag and shows it*) I bought this one last week in (*local card shop*) for a friend of mine. Two pounds fifty, it cost. Two pounds fifty. And all it says is (*reading*) "Here's to a speedy recovery". Mind you, I've been so busy what with one thing and another, I never got around to posting it. So I'm just taking it back to see if they'll change it to one that says "With Deepest Sympathy". (*She sighs*) Oh, but doesn't time go by, girls? Fifty-seven years I've worked in that palace, and if I'm not careful, I'll still be there when I'm thirty. Mind you, as long as I've got *Snow White* to look after I don't really care. (*She remembers*) Oh, but you haven't met *her* yet, have you? Princess Snow White. No, of course you haven't. (*Warmly*) Oh, you'll like her. She's ever so beautiful. In fact, she's the nicest, prettiest girl in the whole wide world. (*Suddenly remembers herself*) Here, but don't let that nasty stepmother of hers, Queen Maligna, know I told you, 'cos if you ask me, she's a bit on the jealous side. Oh, yes. Doesn't like to think anybody's prettier than she is. And talk about unpopular. She's so unpopular, she can take a bath without the phone ringing. Mind you ——

*Alonzo staggers out of the antique shop behind a large, flat package, wrapped in brown paper*

**Alonzo** (*gasping*) Ooooooh. Help. (*He totters c as though about to collapse*)
**Dame** (*startled*) Oh, I say. (*She hurries to assist him*)

*They lower the package to the ground*

**Alonzo** (*panting heavily*) Oh, thank you, Dame Goodheart. Thank you. (*He gasps*) I thought I was going to drop it. It's much heavier than I thought.
**Dame** So I noticed. (*Staring at the package*) What is it?
**Alonzo** Queen Maligna's birthday present. An antique mirror. (*Concerned*) Oh, I do hope she'll like it. It's the most unusual thing I've ever seen. Very old, of course, with mysterious writing all around the edge.
**Dame** Mysterious writing?
**Alonzo** Yes. It says:
  "O gracious owner, 'tis my task
  To answer questions that you ask.
  But heed my warning, ere you try:
  I tell the truth and never lie."
**Dame** (*blinking*) Blimey. Sounds like a politician's speech.
**Alonzo** (*chuckling*) I *did* wonder, perhaps, if … well … if it might be a *magic mirror*. (*He squirms in embarrassment*)

**Dame** Don't be silly, Alonzo. There's no such thing as a magic mirror. (*To the audience*) Is there, girls and boys?

*Audience reaction*

**Alonzo** You see? You see?
**Dame** Well there's one way to find out, isn't there? Let's ask it a question and see what happens.
**Alonzo** (*doubtfully*) Oh, I don't know if we should, Dame Goodheart.
**Dame** Of course we should. You can't give a birthday present to somebody if you don't know whether it's going to work or not. Here, give me a hand.

*They quickly unwrap the mirror*

(*Looking at it*) Oooh, I say … it's not very clean, is it? (*She polishes it with her sleeve*) That's better.
**Alonzo** (*nervously*) Who — er — who's going to ask the question?
**Dame** Well, seeing as you were the one who bought it, I think it's only fair that I should do it. You just stand there and hold it up.

*Alonzo holds the mirror up. Dame stands back and stares into it*

(*Sweetly*) Mirror, mirror, tell me true …
Do I look my age of — *thirty two.*
(*She preens and simpers*)

*The Lights flicker and a deep voice is heard through an off-stage mike*

**Voice of the Spirit** O Mistress, I give answer,
And most heartedly concur.
You do not look the age you give …
Though you *did* do when you *were.*

*The Dame reacts*

**Alonzo** (*wide eyed*) My goodness, it *is* magic.

*Queen Maligna enters* UR. *She is a beautiful but cold and evil person, in robes of black, green and crimson*

**Queen** (*sharply*) Magic? Did I hear the word — "*magic*"? (*She moves* C *between Dame and Alonzo*)
**Alonzo** (*startled*) Your Majesty. (*He attempts to bow*)

*The Dame drops several quick curtsies*

**Queen** (*ignoring her*) Well? (*She fixes Alonzo with a steely glare*)

**Alonzo** (*stammering*) I — I — I was just showing Dame Goodheart the birthday present I'd bought for you, Your Majesty. (*Blurting it out*) A magic mirror.

**Queen** (*sharply*) Magic *mirror*?

**Alonzo** (*backing*) Yes, Your Majesty. It answers any question you ask it. Look. (*He holds it out*)

**Queen** (*reading*) "O gracious owner, 'tis my task …" (*Viciously*) Fool. Dolt. Idiot. You dare offer *me* this pathetic piece of *trash*? I'll have you boiled in oil for the insult. (*Calling*) Guards. Guards.

**Alonzo** (*pleading*) Wait, Your Majesty. Wait. Just try it and see.

**Dame** (*helpfully*) It can't do any harm, can it?

*The Queen glowers for a moment*

**Queen** Very well, then. But if this is a jest, I'll have you *both* exterminated. (*She looks at the mirror. Off-handedly*)
                Mirror, mirror, close at hand,
                Who is the fairest in this land?

*The Lights flicker and the voice is heard once again*

**Voice of the Spirit**    O mighty Queen, accept my word,
                              For what I say is true.
                              There is, in this whole Kingdom,
                              None so beautiful as you.

**Queen** (*astounded*) It's true. I *am* the most beautiful. (*She turns away, gloating*) I am.

**Voice of the Spirit**    Yet very soon, a rival comes
                              To claim your title bright.
                              Her beauty unsurpassable …
                              The young princess, Snow White.

**Queen** (*aghast*) Snow White? (*She turns angrily to face the mirror again*) More beautiful than I? Impossible. You lie. You lie.

*The Lights flicker again*

**Voice of the Spirit**    Each passing hour she grows more fair,
                              Whilst each and ev'ry day
                              *Your* beauty fades, and like the dew,
                              Slips silently away.

**Queen** (*angrily*) Be *silent*, or I'll smash you into a thousand pieces. (*She moves* DL *in an agitated manner*)

**Dame** (*to the audience*) Oh, I say. (*She rolls her eyes*)

**Alonzo** (*quickly*) Take no notice, Your Majesty. Everyone in the kingdom thinks you're as pretty as a picture.

**Dame** (*aside*) Yes. And most of 'em 'd like to hang her.

**Queen** (*to herself*) I won't allow it. Without my beauty I have nothing. (*Thoughtfully*) I must question this mirror more carefully ... but away from the flapping ears of these two idiots. (*She gives a harsh laugh and turns to them*) A toy. 'Tis nothing but a harmless toy. And yet — it *pleases* me. (*Sweetly*) I thank you, dear Alonzo. This gift of yours is gratefully accepted. Take it to my private rooms in the palace and make quite sure that no-one else knows of it. Understand? Not a word to anyone.

**Alonzo** (*relieved*) Yes, Your Majesty. At once, Your Majesty. Immediately.

*He scurries off with the mirror*

**Queen** (*to the Dame*) And as for *you* ... (*Menacingly*) Should the existence of that mirror become known to another soul, I'll feed your tongue to the crows and pickle your eyes in vinegar. Now *go*.

*The Dame quickly exits* DR

So that mewling, whey-faced, stepdaughter of mine will become more beautiful than I, will she? (*She laughs harshly*) We'll see about that.

*She laughs nastily and exits* DL. *As she does so, there is the sound of great hilarity off* L, *and Chuckles, the Court Jester dances on* UR *surrounded by an excited horde of Children. He carries a string of brightly coloured balloons and hands them out as he twirls around*

**Children** (*variously*) One for me, Chuckles. One for me. A blue one. A red one. (*Etc.*)

**Chuckles** (*handing the last one out*) There you are, kids. That's the last. Off you go. See you later.

**Children** (*variously*) Thanks, Chuckles. See you later. 'Bye.

*With much excitement, the Children exit, waving*

*Chuckles waves back, then turns and notices the audience*

**Chuckles** (*moving* C) Ooh, hallo. I didn't notice you sitting out there. Are you tonight's audience, then?

*Audience response*

Oh, smashing. I was hoping we'd get a good looking audience. (*Pause*)
Still, perhaps we'll have better luck tomorrow. (*He laughs*) No, no. Only
joking. You're a lovely looking lot and we're going to have great fun, so
first of all, we'd better get to know each other, hadn't we? (*Brightly*) Right.
Well, my name's Chuckles, and I'm the court jester. That means it's my
job to keep everyone at the palace laughing. Hey, and it's not easy to make
people laugh, you know. Not unless you play football for (*local team*). But
it's a smashing job really, except you don't get any time to make friends.
(*As the thought strikes him*) Here, I bet you could be my friends, couldn't
you?

*Audience response*

Course you could. You could be my bestest friends in the whole wide
world. So I'll tell you what I'll do. Every time I come on, I'm going to shout
"Hiya, kids" and you shout back "Hiya, Chuckles". Will you do that? Will
you?

*Audience response*

All right, then. We'll give it a try. I'll go off and come back on again, and
we'll see what happens.

*He rehearses this with the audience until satisfied*

Smashing. Right. Well, now we're all friends, shall I tell you a secret?

*Audience response*

Shall I?

*Audience response*

All right, then. (*Coyly*) I've got a girlfriend. Yes. And we're madly in love
with each other. Well—*I* am. She doesn't know about it yet. Can you guess
who it is?

*Audience reaction*

Yes. It's Princess Snow White. (*He hugs himself with glee*) Of course ...
that's not her *real* name. Snow White. I mean nobody's called Snow White

for real, are they? Her real name is Princess *Millie*, but everyone calls her Snow White because she's as pretty as a snowflake. (*Dreamily*) She's got big brown eyes, bright rosy cheeks, lovely black hair with curly-whirly ringlets all down her back, and she's the kindest girl in the whole wide world. And ... (*He glances off* UR) Oooh. Here she comes now.

*Snow White enters* UR *to a few bars of musical accompaniment. She is a very pretty girl, with dark hair styled in a neat pageboy bob, and dressed in a blue bodice and knee length yellow skirt with petticoats*

Hiya, Princess. (*He notices her appearance and reacts*) Here, what have you done? What's happened? Your hair, your clothes.

**Snow White** (*amused*) Do you like it, Chuckles? (*She twirls around*)

**Chuckles** (*at a loss*) Well — er — yes. You look smashing. You always do. But — what's that nasty stepmother of yours going to say when she sees you? She'll go potty.

**Snow White** (*laughing*) No, she won't. I don't suppose she'll even notice. (*Ruefully*) I sometimes wonder if she knows I'm here. She's hardly spoken a word to me since Father died.

**Chuckles** Oh, she knows you're there, all right. The trouble is, she's so jealous of you, she can't bear to be in the same room.

**Snow White** (*amazed*) Jealous of *me*? But why?

**Chuckles** Because you're prettier than she is.

*Snow White laughs*

You are. (*To the audience*) Isn't she, kids?

*Audience response*

You see?

**Snow White** (*uncertain*) You really think so?

**Chuckles** Course I do. But — I wish you hadn't cut your hair.

**Snow White** (*amused*) Oh, Chuckles. Don't you understand? I'm grown up now. I want to move with the times. There's a whole new world waiting for me. I don't want to stay in the past forever.

**No. 2** Song (Princess)

*As she sings, Citizens enter, react, then dance or join in the singing*

*At the end of the song, all exit happily. As they do so, Prince Michael enters* UR. *He is richly dressed and carries a gift-wrapped box*

**Prince** (*relieved*) Sylvania, at last. I was starting to think I'd never arrive here. I must have walked miles since my horse lost his shoe in the forest. (*He moves* DC, *glancing around*) Well, it's a pretty enough place, I suppose, and much larger than my own country of Tyrolia, but the sooner I can deliver this birthday present to Queen Maligna and make my excuses, the better. I couldn't bear to attend *another* royal party with pompous old dukes, barons and earls, fawning and flattering and boring everyone to tears. And if Queen Maligna's as bad-tempered as everyone says she is … (*He sighs*) Who'd be a prince in this day and age? (*Cheering up*) Ah, well. I'd better head for the palace and introduce myself. (*He glances around again*) But how do I get there? Perhaps I'd better ask someone.

*Snow White enters, waving to someone off stage as she moves* C

(*Seeing her*) Excuse me.

*She turns to face him*

I'm looking for the royal palace and I — I … (*He stops and gazes at her, lost for words*)
**Snow White** (*after a moment*) Yes?
**Prince** I … (*recovering*) … was wondering if you could give me directions?
**Snow White** (*laughing*) It's easy to see you're a stranger to these parts. Everyone in Sylvania knows where the palace is. (*Kindly*) But there's no need for directions. It's only down the road. (*She indicates* R) I'll take you there, myself.
**Prince** (*happily*) You will? Then permit me to introduce myself. Prince Michael of Tyrolia, at your service. (*He gives a deep, sweeping bow*)
**Snow White** (*surprised*) Prince Michael? Oh … but you're awfully early, aren't you. The party doesn't start until this evening.
**Prince** (*embarrassed*) Well. To tell the truth … I wasn't intending to stay. I just came to deliver this present from my father, King Hildebrand. (*He shows it*) It's supposed to be for Queen Maligna, but … well … I'm sure he must have meant it for you. Look. (*He hands her the package*) Read what it says.
**Snow White** (*reading*) "For the most beautiful lady in all Sylvania".
**Prince** You see? It describes you perfectly.
**Snow White** (*laughing*) But I'm not beautiful.
**Prince** (*earnestly*) You are to me. The most beautiful girl I've ever seen.
**Snow White** (*smiling*) Then it's obvious you've never met Queen Maligna. (*She hands the package back to him*) Once you've seen *her*, you won't give *me* a second thought. (*She turns and moves* DL)

**Prince** Oh, but you're wrong. (*Following her*) And to prove it, I promise to dance with no-one but you at tonight's party. (*Anxiously*) You are going to be there, aren't you?

**Snow White** (*turning to him*) I'm sorry. But my stepmother prefers me to keep out of sight when the palace has visitors.

**Prince** (*frowning*) Does she indeed? Well, don't worry about *her*. I'll ask the Queen, herself, to invite her.

**Snow White** (*shaking her head*) You don't understand. Queen Maligna *is* my stepmother.

**Prince** (*surprised*) Oh.

**Snow White** I'm Princess Millie ... (*shyly*) ... though all my friends call me Snow White.

**Prince** (*dreamily*) Snow White. What a beautiful name.

**Snow White** (*suddenly anxious*) But I'd better be getting back. I promised to help in the kitchen with all the cooking.

**Prince** (*aghast*) Help in the kitchen? A royal princess helping in the *kitchen*?

**Snow White** (*quickly*) Oh, it's all right. I enjoy doing it. And thanks to Dame Goodheart, I can cook almost anything now.

**Prince** (*protesting*) But you shouldn't be hidden away in a kitchen on a lovely day like this. Today's a day to be enjoying yourself. (*Suddenly*) Why not show me around Sylvania, instead?

**Snow White** (*regretfully*) I wish I could ... but there's such a lot to do at the palace.

**Prince** Are you sure you can't be persuaded?

### No. 3 Song (Prince)

*At the end of the song, they move off together*

*The Lights fade to a Black-out*

### SCENE 2

*A corridor in the palace*

*The Dame enters* R, *in a garish gown*

**Dame** (*excitedly*) Oh, I say, boys and girls. Isn't it exciting? Everybody's arriving for the party and you can't move in the courtyard for carriages. (*Worried*) Oh, I hope I've done enough food. I've not moved from that kitchen all afternoon. Well ... I daren't. As fast as I've taken the cakes out of the oven, people have been eating 'em. (*Coyly*) Mind you ... it's very flattering when a girl gets to my age, and fellers are still trying to get their hands on her "Fancies". (*She chortles*) Here, and speaking of fancy, what do you think of the frock? (*She parades it*) I bought it for tonight's party. From (*she names a local dress shop*). Mind you, I won't be going there again in a hurry. I mean, I've heard of being helpful, but they're ridiculous. I went in and said "Excuse me, but I'd like you to put me in something long and flowing", and before I could move a muscle, they'd chucked me in the river. (*She glances off* L) Oh, I say — here comes Chuckles, the love of my life. Let's see if *he* notices it. (*Quickly she assumes what she supposes to be a romantic posture, head thrown back, hand on hip*)

*Chuckles enters* L

**Chuckles** (*to the audience*) Hiya, kids. (*Seeing the Dame*) Oh, no. You've not twisted your back again, have you?

**Dame** (*annoyed*) No, I haven't twisted me back. I was giving you one of my famous "come hither" looks. (*Proudly*) The last feller I looked at like that nearly passed out at me feet.

**Chuckles** I'm not surprised. I felt a bit sick, meself. Anyway, what are you doing out here? Shouldn't you be in the kitchen getting all the food ready?

**Dame** It *is* ready. (*Smugly*) Snow White and that new boyfriend of hers have been helping me.

**Chuckles** (*startled*) *What* new boyfriend?

**Dame** Prince Michael, of course. (*Gleefully*) Here, and he's ever so good-looking, you know. Just like (*famous personage*).

**Chuckles** Never mind about that. Where did *he* come from? I thought *I* was Snow White's boyfriend.

**Dame** You? (*scornfully*) Don't be daft. You don't get beautiful princesses running around with court jesters. They want fellers with brains and ambition.

**Chuckles** (*indignantly*) I've got brains and ambition. I'm going to be a writer, I am. I've been writing a book for the last ten years.

**Dame** (*incredulously*) Well that just shows how daft you are, then, doesn't it? (*Scornfully*) Fancy wasting all that time writing a book. For a few pounds, you could have gone into (*local bookshop*) and bought one already written.

**Chuckles** (*despairingly*) Oh, you don't understand. If I can't marry Snow White, there's nothing left to live for. I might as well throw myself in the river and drown. (*He turns to exit*)

**Dame** (*startled*) Here. Wait a minute. There's no need to do that. If you're looking for someone to marry, why don't you marry *me*? (*She attempts to look coy*)

**Chuckles** No, no. I couldn't marry you, Dame Goodheart. Not after the things *I've* been hearing.

**Dame** (*surprised*) What things?

**Chuckles** Well ... last Friday night, for instance. Down in (*local street*). A strange man grabbed you and started kissing you, and *you* never said a word.

**Dame** Of course I didn't. My mother told me not to speak to strange men.

**Chuckles** And what about the milkman, eh? You let *him* put his arm around you *three times*.

**Dame** (*disdainfully*) Don't be silly. Nobody's got an arm *that* long. (*Coaxing*) Oh, come on, Chuckles. Ask me to marry you. Ask me to marry you. All my life I've wanted to be wooed. (*She puckers her lips at him*)

**Chuckles** (*recoiling*) Yes ... well you needn't get wooed with me.

**Dame** (*to the audience*) That's what I like about this one: he's got an answer for everything. (*To Chuckles*) Come here, you little sex-pot, you.

**No. 4** Song (Dame and Chuckles)

*At the end of the song, the Dame chases Chuckles off* R. *As they go, Queen Maligna enters* L, *angrily*

**Queen** Impossible. Absolutely impossible. For hours I've questioned the magic mirror, yet *still* it insists Snow White will soon be more beautiful than I. (*Furious*) Never. Never in a million years. I'll choke her to death with my own fair hands before I allow it to happen. (*To the audience*) Oh, shut up, or I'll poison the drinks for the Interval. (*Calling*) Chamberlain. Lord Chamberlain.

*Alonzo enters* R, *hurriedly*

**Alonzo** (*breathlessly*) You called, Your Majesty?

**Queen** Of course I did, you bumbling buffoon. Where is the princess, Snow White? (*Scornfully*) Out in the forest, gathering flowers again, I suppose? (*She scowls and moves* L)

**Alonzo** (*shocked*) Oh, no, Your Majesty. Certainly not. The forest isn't safe at the moment. Only this morning, your royal huntsman was attacked by a savage wolf.

**Queen** (*sharply*) Wolf? (*She turns to face him*)

**Alonzo** (*nodding rapidly*) A monstrous creature, with eyes like red hot coals and teeth like daggers. The poor man barely escaped with his life.

**Queen** (*eyes narrowing*) And the *wolf*?

**Alonzo** Still free, Your Majesty. (*He looks most unhappy*) Still free.

**Queen** (*thoughtfully*) I see. (*Aside*) This could be my chance to get rid of this simpering child once and for all. (*Aloud*) Who else knows of this ravenous wolf, Lord Chamberlain?

**Alonzo** (*wide eyed*) Hardly anyone, Your Majesty. (*Quickly*) But I'm about to send the Town Crier out to warn them.

**Queen** (*soothingly*) No, no, Alonzo. There's no need for that. We don't want to frighten them, do we? Especially on my birthday. Besides, it will probably be miles away by now. (*She smiles sweetly*)

**Alonzo** (*protesting*) But, Your Majesty ——

**Queen** (*sharply*) Enough. Tell the princess I wish to have words with her. And remember, not a word about the wolf to anyone. (*She indicates for him to go*)

*Alonzo bows unhappily and bustles off R*

(*Gleefully*) At last. The perfect way to get rid of that cursed Snow White — and not a finger of suspicion to point in my direction. (*With mock regret*) Poor child. Torn to pieces by a fearsome wolf whilst wandering alone in the great forest. (*She laughs wickedly and snarls savagely*) I'll show that stupid mirror how wrong it can be. No-one shall surpass the beauty of Queen Maligna. (*Fiercely*) No-one.

*Snow White enters R*

**Snow White** You wanted me, Stepmother?

*The Queen turns to see her, and reacts*

**Queen** (*shocked*) Your hair. Your clothes.

**Snow White** (*brightly*) Do you like them? (*She twirls around*)

**Queen** (*dazed*) Such beauty. Such terrible beauty. (*Recovering herself*) Very pretty, my dear, but the guests are already arriving, so I think it's time to go to your room, don't you?

**Snow White** (*hopefully*) Couldn't I stay and watch, Stepmother? Just for once. I promise I won't be a nuisance.

**Queen** (*laughing gaily*) Perhaps next year, darling. (*Aside; savagely*) If you live that long. (*To Snow White*) Besides, you'll need a good night's sleep before tomorrow's big adventure, won't you? (*She smiles sweetly*)

**Snow White** (*blankly*) Big adventure?

**Queen** (*brightly*) But, of course. First thing in the morning, we're going for a special little picnic in the great forest — just you and I. And once we're there, you can show me all the secret places where the prettiest flowers grow. (*She smiles*) Won't that be fun? (*She turns away and grimaces*)

**Snow White** (*doubtfully*) I — suppose so.

**Queen** Then off you go, precious one. And — pleasant dreams.

*Snow White reluctantly exits*

(*Savagely*) The little fool. She'll never leave that forest alive. (*She laughs nastily*) And now to the royal ballroom to meet my guests.

*She glares at the audience and exits laughing*

*The Lights fade to a Black-out*

SCENE 3

*The Great Ballroom*

*Upstage, on a small dais, is an ornate throne. This scene should be as spectacular as possible*

*Noblemen and their Ladies, dressed in rich, glittering costumes, dance a grand gavotte*

**No. 5** Dance (Nobility)

*At the end of the dance, the dancers break into small groups and chat silently*

*Chuckles enters* UR *in his "posh" jester's outfit*

**Chuckles** (*calling*) Hiya, kids. (*He moves downstage* C) Cor, doesn't it look posh, here? It's just like (*local restaurant*). Everybody dressed in their Sunday Best, and champagne flowing like water. If they'd spent another few thousand, it'd be almost as good as (*local Council*) Annual Dinner and Dance. (*He chortles*) Mind you, they're all rich in Sylvania, you know. Even the *pigeons* have got money. Well, they must have, mustn't they? I mean, there's a couple of 'em up on the roof, and I just heard one of 'em saying to the other : "Here, Bert, there's a brand new Rolls Royce in the courtyard. Let's fly down and put a deposit on it". (*He chortles*)

*The Dame enters* UR *in an outrageous costume*

**Dame** (*seeing him*) Yoo-hoo. (*She moves down to him, beaming broadly*)
**Chuckles** (*admiringly*) Here, I say, that's an unusual frock you're wearing, Dame Goodheart. Makes you look like a Charlotte Noisette.
**Dame** (*flattered; to the audience*) Ohhhh! Did you hear that, boys and girls? He thinks I look like a Charlotte Noisette. (*She preens, then realizes*) Hang on a minute. A Charlotte Noisette's a fruity, old-fashioned tart that's half nuts.

**Chuckles** That's right. (*He chortles*)
**Dame** (*playfully pushing him*) Saucebox. (*Beaming*) Oh, I am looking forward to tonight. They've got some really unusual entertainment laid on. (*Proudly*) A bungee-jumping team from (*local area*). (*Eyes sparkling*) They're going to join hands and leap six hundred feet from the top of the North Tower.
**Chuckles** What's unusual about that? Everybody's bungee jumping these days.
**Dame** Yes. But not without ropes. (*Excitedly*) Here, why don't you have a go, as well?
**Chuckles** (*recoiling*) No fear. I might have an accident.
**Dame** (*airily*) So what? Everybody has a little accident, now and then.
**Chuckles** (*firmly*) Not me. I've never had an accident in my life.
**Dame** (*surprised*) I beg your pardon. What about last year when you went into Farmer Brown's field and his bull tossed you over the hedge? Don't you call that an accident?
**Chuckles** Course I don't. It did that on purpose.

*Prince Michael enters* R

**Prince** (*seeing them*) Dame Goodheart. (*He moves towards them*)
**Dame** (*to Chuckles*) Oooh, I say, it's Prince Michael. Keep quiet and I'll seduce you to him. (*To the Prince; fussily*) Hallo, Prinny. (*She indicates Chuckles*) This is Chuckles, my latest fiasco. (*She flutters*)
**Prince** (*frowning*) Don't you mean *fiancée*?
**Dame** *I* know what I mean.
**Prince** (*warmly*) Hallo, Chuckles. I've heard so much about you. It must be wonderful to make people laugh. I wish I could do it.
**Chuckles** (*sourly*) Yes. Well with legs like yours, you shouldn't have any problems, should you?

*The Prince looks surprised. The Dame glares at Chuckles, then turns to the Prince again*

**Dame** Treat him with ignoramus, dear. He's just jealous because Snow White prefers you to him.
**Prince** (*concerned*) Oh, I hope not. Because if she'll marry me, I want Chuckles to be the best man at our wedding — and you, Dame Goodheart, to be the Matron of Honour.
**Dame** (*overcome*) Oh, I say. Did you hear that, Chuckles? Best man and Matron of Honour. I've always wanted to be a Matron of Honour. (*To the Prince*) Oh, thank you. Thank you from the bottom of my heart. (*She remembers and indicates Chuckles*) And thank you from *his* bottom, as well.

**Prince** (*glancing around*) But where is she? I don't see her anywhere.
**Chuckles** (*sulkily*) No. And you're not going to, either. She's up in her room getting ready for bed.
**Prince** (*surprised*) But — but she'd agreed to meet me here.
**Chuckles** Yes, well, you're out of luck, Mr Smartypants, 'cos Queen Maligna had *other* ideas. (*He cocks a snook*)
**Dame** (*pushing him; indignantly*) Here, don't you be so rude.
**Chuckles** (*defensively*) Well …

*There is a fanfare*

*Alonzo enters* UL *to take up a position* UC. *He carries his rod of office, which he grandly pounds on the floor to attract attention*

**Alonzo** (*announcing*) Her Glorious Majesty, Queen Maligna of Sylvania.

*The Prince, Dame and Chuckles move* DR. *All bow or curtsy deeply*

*Queen Maligna enters* UL

*The orchestra strikes up "Happy Birthday" and all sing as she haughtily parades herself before ascending the dais*

**Queen** (*grandly*) Greetings, Loyal subjects — and welcome to the royal palace …(*She gazes around at them in a superior manner*)
**Prince** (*aside to the Dame*) I'm going to speak to her.

*As the Dame reacts in dismay, he crosses to the Queen*

Your Majesty. (*He bows deeply*)

*Everyone looks at him*

**Queen** (*imperiously*) And who are *you*?
**Prince** (*proudly*) Prince Michael of Tyrolia, Your Majesty. Son of King Hildebrand the Steadfast.

*Everyone reacts*

**Queen** (*softening*) Prince Michael. (*Descending the dais and moving to him graciously*) My, how you've grown. You were only a child when I saw you last. Whoever dreamed you'd turn out to be … (*she smiles at him, seductively*) … so handsome. (*She caresses his cheek with her hand*)

**Prince** Your Majesty is kind. But I beg of you. Grant me a favour.

**Queen** (*archly*) Whatever could *that* be, I wonder? (*She moves downstage*)

**Prince** When I first arrived in Sylvania, my only desire was to leave again as soon as possible. But that was before I met the most beautiful girl in all the world — and completely lost my heart to her.

**Queen** (*thinking he means her*) Such flattery. (*She smirks at the guests*)

**Prince** (*earnestly*) Not if you could see her through *my* eyes, Your Majesty. She's the girl I've dreamed of meeting for as long as I can remember — and the one I intend to claim as my future bride.

**Queen** (*smiling*) I see. And the favour you seek of me? (*She preens*)

**Prince** Permission to dance with her for the entire evening.

**Queen** (*amused*) Such a simple request. How can I possibly refuse?

**Prince** Then — you've no objection?

**Queen** (*graciously*) You shall dance to your heart's delight.

*The Prince throws a quick look at the Dame whose face lights up*

*The Dame hurries off* R *quickly*

(*Imperiously*) Let the music begin. (*She holds out her hand for the Prince to take*)

*The Guests begin to take up positions*

**Prince** (*quickly*) But Your Majesty. She hasn't arrived yet.

*The Queen's smile becomes fixed and her hand drops*

**Queen** (*harshly*) She?

**Prince** Your royal stepdaughter. The Princess Snow White.

**Queen** (*disbelievingly*) You wish to dance with *Snow White*?

**Prince** More than anything else in the world. Dame Goodheart's gone to find her. (*He glances off* R)

**Queen** (*icily*) How *dare* she leave the ball without asking my permission?

**Chuckles** (*cheerily*) Oh, she's not very musical, Dame Goodheart. Can't tell one tune from another. Remember the last dance you had here? We spent all night arguing about what the band was playing. *She* said it was "Phil the Fluter's Ball", and *I* said it was "Rock Around the Clock".

**Prince** And who was right?

**Chuckles** Neither of us. We looked at the little notice board on the edge of the band-stand, and according to that, it was the Refrain from Spitting.

*Snow White enters* UR *in a dazzling ball gown and moves downstage*

*The Guests applaud and gaze at her in admiration. The Queen glares at her in fury, though tries to mask her feelings*

*The Dame enters behind Snow White and moves to stand beside Chuckles*

**Prince** (*overwhelmed*) Your Highness. (*He takes Snow White's hand and kisses it*)
**Dame** (*to Chuckles, with feeling*) Oh, isn't it romantic?

*Chuckles scowls and looks away*

**Snow White** (*crossing to the Queen, happily*) Oh, thank you for letting me come to the ball, Stepmother. (*She kisses her on the cheek*)
**Queen** (*forcing a smile*) Not at all, my dear. Run along and enjoy yourself.

*As Snow White turns back to the Prince, the Queen wipes away the kiss savagely*

(*Aside*) It's the last chance you'll ever get. (*Aloud*) Musicians.

*The music begins to play. Everyone takes their partners for the dance*

**No. 6** Song (Prince, Snow White and Company)

*The Queen swirls about and exits DL, unnoticed by the crowd as they sing and dance*

*At the end of the song, there is general merriment as the Lights fade rapidly to a Black-out*

SCENE 4

*A Corridor in the Queen's Private Chambers*

*The Queen enters L in a fury and moves C*

**Queen** How *dare* he insult me in my own Court! How dare he reject *me* to dance with that snivelling brat, Snow White! (*Scornfully*) The boy's a fool. An idiot. Her vapid features are *nothing* compared to *my* dazzling beauty. (*Cooing*) Who else has skin as soft and creamy as mine? Eyes so large and dark? Lips redder than the reddest rose that blooms in the palace gardens? (*Smirking*) No-one. (*Fiercely*) No-one. (*She swirls around to face L, declaiming*) Mirror, mirror, on the wall, who is the fairest of them all?

*The Lights flicker and the Spirit's voice is heard*

**Voice of the Spirit**    Thy beauty, mighty Queen, is greater
Than the star-filled night.
Yet ten times ten more greater now
Is that of young Snow White.

**Queen**    (*recoiling*) Aaaaaagh. (*Savagely*) How I *hate* the sound of that accursed name. Even in my *dreams*, I hear it whispered. Snow White. Snow White. Snow White. (*Pulling herself together*) But calmly. Calmly. Why should I worry? By this time tomorrow her bones will be rotting in the forest and I, Queen Maligna, will once again be the most beautiful woman on earth. (*She laughs harshly*)

*Alonzo hurries in* L, *flushed with excitement*

**Alonzo**    Oh, Your Majesty. Wonderful news. Simply *wonderful*. The wolf in the Great Forest. It's been killed. By a village wood-cutter. (*He beams at her in delight*)

**Queen**    (*stunned*) What?

**Alonzo**    (*happily*) He's just bought it into the courtyard to show us and he claims the traditional reward.

**Queen**    (*turning away in a fury; muttering to herself*) Confound the stupid peasant. Are my plans to be thwarted at every turn? (*Controlling herself; turning back to Alonzo*) Very well, give him ten pieces of gold and send the royal huntsman to me at once.

**Alonzo**    (*flustered*) Oh. But has Your Majesty forgotten? The poor man is still on his sick bed and not expected to live.

**Queen**    (*frustrated*) Then send me — (*as the thought strikes her*) — that idiot of a *jester*, Chuckles. And hurry.

**Alonzo**    (*hastily*) Yes, Your Majesty. At once, Your Majesty.

*Alonzo exits* L

**Queen**    (*grimly*) Nothing shall save her, I swear it. Nothing. If she cannot be killed by the teeth and claws of a wolf, then she'll die at the hands of a man. (*She smiles coldly*) And who better to do it than her dearest friend, Chuckles? (*She laughs nastily*)

*Chuckles enters* R

**Chuckles**    Hiya, kids.

*Audience response*

**Queen**    (*sweetly*) Ah, Chuckles. My faithful jester. Tell me something ... (*Smiling at him*) How would you like to be my new royal huntsman?

**Chuckles** (*taken aback*) Eh? (*Quickly*) Oh, I don't think so, Mrs Queen. I
don't know anything about animals, I don't. Nothing at all.
**Queen** You mean ... you've never taken a gun into the forest and hunted
bear?
**Chuckles** No. (*Remembering*) But I've taken a stick and a jar of worms and
gone fishing in my underpants.
**Queen** (*unamused*) No matter, the job is yours. First thing tomorrow you'll
go into the wood and catch a deer for Sunday lunch.
**Chuckles** (*dismayed*) But—but—I might get lost. All on my own in a place
like that. It's all dark and gloomy.
**Queen** (*pretending to think*) How very true. Then why not take Snow White
with you? She often goes to the forest to gather flowers, and knows its paths
like the back of her hand. (*Brightly*) Why ... you could even take a picnic.
I'm sure Dame Goodheart will be only too pleased to arrange one for you.
**Chuckles** (*brightening*) Oooh, yes. (*To the audience*) And it'd get her away
from that rotten Prince Michael, as well, wouldn't it? I could be with her
all on me *own*. (*He grins with delight, then turns to the Queen again*). Right,
Mrs Queen. You've got yourself a new huntsman. (*He beams*)
**Queen** (*triumphant*) Splendid. (*Eyes narrowing*) Then from now on, you do
everything I tell you to. Without question. Without hesitation. And should
you fail me ... (*She draws her finger across her throat*)
**Chuckles** (*gulping, then recovering*) Don't worry, Mrs Queen. I won't let
you down. Anything you want. Just ask me.
**Queen** Then find yourself a sharp knife and meet me here tomorrow *at dawn*.

*Chuckles exits* R

(*Triumphantly*)  Come dazzling sun,
                 And sweep away the night.
                 The deed will very soon be done ...
                 And death will claim Snow White.

*The Queen shrieks with laughter and exits* L

*The Lights fade to a Black-out*

SCENE 5

*The Great Forest. Morning*

*There is a backdrop of dense forest, and mountains with tree flats* L *and* R *and
a slightly raised grassy mound* UL

*Dappled, morning light is shining through the trees. The Juniors as Forest
Game perform a dance (optional)*

**No. 7** Dance (Juniors)

*Soft music ripples as the Fairy enters* R, *in a white follow spot*

**Fairy** (*to the audience*)  Within this mighty forest's shade,
The next scene of our tale is played.
For here, despite the Queen's intention,
Kind fate makes an intervention,
To prove the proverb "many a slip
Is made between the cup and lip."
So where the songbirds sweetly call,
Begins Maligna's *own* downfall.

*The Fairy exits* R

**Dame** (*off* L) Yoo-hoo. Chuckles. Snow Whi-ite. Are you there, dears?

*The Dame enters* UL, *carrying a picnic basket*

(*Seeing the audience*) Oh, I say, you haven't seen Snow White and Chuckles anywhere, have you?

*Audience response*

They went off so early this morning, they forgot to take their picnic basket. (*Displaying it*) They'll be absolutely starving by lunchtime. (*She sighs*) Still, I suppose I can eat it myself if I don't find 'em. I mean, I've nothing to rush back to the palace for — and it's been years since I had a picnic in the forest. In fact the *last* time I was here, I came with (*famous male personage*). Here, and I'll tell you *this*, boys and girls. That man is so intelligent, he can speak over fifty different languages. (*Nodding*) Yes. You wouldn't believe it, would you? Fifty different languages. (*Smugly*) He told me how much he fancied me in *three* of 'em. French — Italian — and Braille. (*She chortles*) Mind you ——

*Alonzo enters* L

**Alonzo** (*beaming*) Ah, there you are, Dame Goodheart.
**Dame** (*dismayed*) Oh, no. What are *you* doing here? How did you find me?
**Alonzo** (*happily*) Quite simple. I've been treading in your footsteps all morning.
**Dame** (*sniffing suspiciously*) Well you've definitely been treading in *something*. (*She wrinkles her nose and snorts in disgust*) Pooooh.

*Alonzo hastily checks the soles of his shoes, grimaces and scrapes his foot on the ground*

Anyway, what do you want? Don't say old misery-guts needs me back at the palace.

**Alonzo** (*hastily*) Oh, no, no, no. It's nothing like that. I just happened to see you leaving the palace with your picnic basket, and couldn't resist following you. (*Dreamily*) You know, drink does so much for you, Dame Goodheart. It really does. It makes you look tender — fragile — melting and beautiful.

**Dame** (*flattered*) Oh, I say ... (*She blinks and frowns*) Hang on a minute. What are you talking about? I haven't been drinking.

**Alonzo** No — but I have. That's why I followed you.

**Dame** (*grimly*) I see. And you want to get all romantic with me, do you? You want to get me alone and put your big, muscular arms around me waist and cover me with hot, searing, kisses and make mad, passionate, abandoned love to me. That's what you want. Isn't it?

**Alonzo** (*startled*) Certainly not. I wouldn't dream of it.

**Dame** (*regretfully*) That's a pity. (*Brightening*) Still, it's a good job, really, 'cos I like my fellers to have a military background. You know, the kind of men who've got good war records.

**Alonzo** (*modestly*) Well, I've got one of *those*.

**Dame** (*startled*) Eh? (*In disbelief*) You've got a war record?

**Alonzo** Yes. It's the Andrews Sisters singing "Roll Out the Barrel".

**Dame** (*to the audience*) Isn't he a treasure? I think I'll have him buried. (*To Alonzo, annoyed*) Well, what *do* you want, then?

**Alonzo** Just the pleasure of your company — and perhaps a nibble on your excellent comestibles.

**Dame** (*to the audience*) Blimey. *That's* the best offer I've had this week. (*To Alonzo*) You mean, all you want is to share what's in this basket?

**Alonzo** (*nodding*) I'm the only one with nothing to eat, you see. The others have brought their own.

**Dame** (*baffled*) What others?

*The Citizens enter carrying picnic baskets and hampers, etc.*

(*Dismayed*) What are *they* doing here?

*The Citizens form small groups around the perimeters of the clearing, and chatter animatedly but silently*

**Alonzo** (*blissfully*) It was such a lovely day, I invited them to join us. I just *knew* you wouldn't mind. (*To the Citizens*) Come along, everyone, baskets down. It's time to *enjoy* ourselves.

*The Dame rolls her eyes in disbelief and quickly exits R unnoticed, as the song begins*

**No. 8** Song and Dance (Alonzo and Citizens)

*At the end of the routine, all move back to perimeters, happy and exhausted*

*Prince Michael enters* L

**Prince**  (*seeing Alonzo*) Lord Chamberlain. (*He hurries to him*) Thank goodness I've found you. Where's Snow White? I've just *got* to speak to her. (*He glances around for a glimpse of her*)

**Alonzo**  (*surprised*) She's not with *us*, Your Highness.

*All shake their heads and agree*

**Prince**  (*baffled*) But she *must* be. Queen Maligna said she was in the forest. Having a picnic.

**Alonzo**  (*puzzled*) Really? Well, none of *us* have seen her.

*Again, all agree*

**Prince**  (*pleading*) Then what am I going to do? I have to return home this morning, and I promised to see her before I went. (*Puzzled*) Why on earth didn't she wait?

**Alonzo**  (*brightly*) I've no idea, Sire. But don't worry. If she's here in the forest, I'm sure *we* can find her for you. (*To the Citizens*) Come along, everyone. She can't be too far away.

*They all begin to gather up their things in preparation for leaving*

*Queen Maligna enters* DL

**Queen**  (*sharply*) Wait.

*All turn to look at her and quickly drop to one knee or curtsy*

There's no need to search for Snow White. I know exactly where she is. Return to the palace at once — all of you. Prince Michael and I have to speak in private.

**Prince**  (*puzzled*) We do?

**Queen**  There's something you need to know. Something important. (*To the others, harshly*) Quickly.

*Alonzo and the Citizens hastily rise and exit*

(*With affected sympathy*) Poor Prince Michael. How I wish there were an easier way to tell you this. (*She gives him a sidelong glance*)

**Prince** (*puzzled*) Tell me what?
**Queen** (*with mock sympathy*) Poor Michael, I should have warned you last night. This isn't the first time she's played her cruel tricks on a handsome prince. (*She turns away, smirking*)
**Prince** I don't believe it.
**Queen** (*turning to face him; innocently*) Would I lie to you. She asked *me* to tell you that she never wanted to see you again.
**Prince** (*protesting*) But you said she'd gone for a picnic. In the forest.
**Queen** And so she has, with her *new* beloved — Chuckles, my court jester. (*She moves to him affecting sympathy again*)
**Prince** (*downcast*) Then — she never loved me at all?
**Queen** (*gently*) Never. You were just a passing fancy. A plaything to be tossed aside as soon as she'd tired of you. And now you know the truth, I suggest you return to Tyrolia and forget all about her. You'll find a *far* worthier bride in your *own* country, of that I'm certain. (*In mock regret*) But alas. Duty calls. I must return to the palace and matters of State. (*She moves away*) Goodbye, Michael dear. I trust you'll have a safe journey home.

*The Queen exits* L, *with a triumphant smirk*

**Prince** (*brokenly*) Snow White. I thought you loved me. I really did.

**No. 9** Song (Prince)

*After the song, he exits slowly* DL

*A moment later, Chuckles can be heard off* R

**Chuckles** (*off, calling*) Princess. Princess. Wait.

*Snow White hurries in* UR, *clutching a small posy of wild flowers, and moves* C, *looking around anxiously. She is followed closely by Chuckles, who has a large dagger tucked in his belt*

(*To the audience*) Hiya, kids. (*To Snow White, breathlessly*) Blimey. What did you want to go running off like that for?
**Snow White** It was Michael, Chuckles. Prince Michael. I heard his voice. (*She moves* DL, *gazing around*) He must be looking for me to say farewell.
**Chuckles** (*shaking his head*) No, he isn't. He'll be halfway home by now. (*Disgusted*) Rushing to tell his dad that he's going to get married. (*Baffled*) Honestly, I don't know what you see in him, Princess. (*Smugly*) He's not half as good-looking as I am.
**Snow White** (*kindly*) I know, Chuckles — but I love him. He's charming, and kind, and witty — and he even speaks a foreign language.

**Chuckles** Well … What's special about that? Don't you remember last year when you had your birthday and *I* took you out to dinner? We went to a real posh restaurant, didn't we? And it didn't half surprise that snooty waiter when I ordered the whole meal in *French*.

**Snow White** I surprised *me*, too. It was a *Chinese* restaurant.

**Chuckles** (*suddenly*) Here — and talking about food. I still haven't caught a deer for Sunday lunch and your stepmother's going to go potty if all we go back with is a bunch of wild flowers.

**Snow White** (*sighing*) That's true. But we haven't seen one all morning. (*She yawns*) Oh, dear. We were up so early, this fresh air's making me sleepy. Do you think we could rest for a little while?

**Chuckles** (*kindly*) Course we can. I'll tell you what. You go have a lie down over there — (*he indicates the mound*) — and I'll gather some berries for lunchtime.

**Snow White** (*gratefully*) Oh, Chuckles. You're so kind to me. (*She moves to the mound*)

**Chuckles** (*embarrassed*) Well — I promised your dad, didn't I? I told him I'd always look after you, no matter what happened.

*Snow White settles herself on the mound*

And even if you *do* want to marry that rotten old Prince Michael, I'm still going to do it. (*Facing front, firmly*) He knew he could trust me. I'll follow his instructions to the very letter. (*Suddenly*) Oooooh. (*He frantically pats his body, then produces an envelope from his tunic with a sigh of relief*) I nearly forgot this. It's the letter Queen Maligna gave me this morning. She said I had to open it when we got to the middle of the forest. (*Puzzled*) I wonder what it is? Shall I open it now? (*He turns to look at Snow White*)

*Snow White is asleep*

Princess? (*Realizing*) Oh, she's asleep. Well, we must be in the middle of the forest now. (*He opens the envelope and takes out a letter. Reading aloud*) "My dearest faithful Chuckles" … (*To the audience*) Ooh, I say. (*Reading*) "By this time, you will be all alone in the forest depths." (*To the audience*) Yes, we are, aren't we? There's nobody else here. (*Reading*) "Now take out your dagger —" (*To the audience*) Take out my dagger. (*He takes the dagger out, then reads on in dawning horror*) "— kill the princess and bring me her repulsive heart that I may gleefully rejoice. Fail to do this, and I will tear out your own heart with my bare hands. No-one shall be fairer than I. Signed, Queen Maligna." (*He lowers the letter in disbelief*) Kill Snow White? She must be crackers. (*Worried*) I can't do that, can I, kids?

*Audience response*

Oooooh, what am I going to do? (*He starts to cry*)

*The Dame enters with the picnic basket*

**Dame** (*seeing him*) Oh, *there* you are. I've been traipsing all over the forest looking for you. I've brought some ... (*Anxiously*) Here. What's wrong? What is it?

*He hands her the letter and she reads it*

(*Looking up, aghast*) Well, the nasty old witch. She can't get away with this. (*Grimly*) I *knew* I didn't like her, the first time I met her. There she was, standing outside the Oxfam shop in (*local town*) scratching her head and picking her teeth.

**Chuckles** (*sniffling*) And what happened?

**Dame** What do you think happened? She went in and bought 'em. (*Suddenly worried*) Oh, poor Snow White. What's she going to *do*? She can't go back to the palace. Not if the queen wants her dead.

**Chuckles** (*tearfully*) Neither can I. (*He wipes at his eyes*)

**Dame** (*firmly*) Oh yes you *can*. But we're going to need Snow White's help. Quick, let's wake her up.

*They hurry to the mound and wake up Snow White*

**Snow White** (*startled*) Dame Goodheart. Chuckles. What is it?

**Dame** That nasty stepmother of yours has told Chuckles to kill you and cut your heart out.

**Chuckles** (*miserably*) And if I don't do it, she's going to kill *me*.

**Snow White** (*horrified*) But why? (*Rising*) I don't understand.

**Dame** Because she's *jealous* of you, dear, that's why. (*Kindly*) But don't you worry. Nobody's going to hurt you. Me and Chuckles have got a plan.

**Chuckles** (*blankly*) Have we?

**Dame** Of course we have. (*To Snow White*) You set off through the forest and find that Prince Michael of yours in Tyrolia. Tell him what's happened, and you can bet your life that he'll see old tricky-knickers gets exactly what's coming to her. And while you're doing that, me and Chuckles'll go back to the palace and pretend he's done what she told him to do, so that way, she'll never find out you're still alive till it's too late. (*She nods in satisfaction*)

**Chuckles** (*miserably*) But what about her heart? I'm supposed to cut it out and take it with me.

**Dame** Oh, don't worry about that. I've got a nice big sheep's heart in the kitchen. You can give her that. She'll never know the difference. (*To Snow White, tearfully*) Take care, lovie. (*She hugs her*) And hurry as fast as you can.

**Chuckles** (*sadly*) Cheerio, Princess. (*He hugs her*) We're going to miss you.
**Snow White**  It won't be for long, Chuckles. I know it won't. I'll be back
before you know it.
**Dame**  (*giving her the basket*) Take this. Now hurry, Snow White. Hurry.

*Snow White hurries off* R

**Chuckles** (*calling*) 'Bye, Princess. 'Bye. (*He bursts into tears again*)
**Dame** (*impatiently*) Oh, shut up. We've got to get back to the palace and find
that sheep's heart. Now come on.

*She grabs his arm and marches him off* DL

*The Lights slowly dim and continue throughout the following*

*The Fairy enters* R

**Fairy**                    As down the twisting forest paths,
                             Snow White, on weary footsteps sped,
                             That night, between her goose-down quilts,
                             Maligna dreamed the girl lay dead.
                             But fairy magic kept her safe
                             From savage tooth and claw,
                             And led her into woodland depths
                             She'd never seen before.
                             A place of great tranquillity,
                             A haven of delight,
                             Where guardians of the forest danced
                             Throughout the moonlit night.

*The lighting slowly changes to moonlight and soft mist sweeps across the
floor*

                             So ere our interval begins,
                             That scene we now display —
                             And fairy revels charm your eye
                             Until the break of day.

*The Forest Fairies enter and perform a graceful ballet*

**No. 10** Dance (Fairies)

*At the end of the dance, the Principal Fairy is* C, *with others in attitudes
around her*

CURTAIN

# ACT II

## SCENE 1

*A Cottage in the Forest. Day*

*A cottage interior, quaint and stylized, with carved wooden beams, fire-place, etc. Mullioned windows look out on to thick forest. A raised landing, about three feet wide, runs R to L, across the back, and on this are seven small beds, with roughly carved foot and headboards, each having a pillow and faded patchwork quilt. All of the beds have been slept in and need remaking. A set of three rickety wooden stairs lead up to this landing. A roughly carved table is C, and around it are seven rickety wooden chairs to match. On the table is a dirty cloth, seven small bowls with wooden spoons, seven beakers, a cracked milk jug, a large ceramic teapot, an open butter dish, a buttery knife, a wooden bread board, half a cottage loaf and a bread knife. A carved broom with a straw head is propped up against a wall. A basket of dirty washing is DL*

*As the* CURTAIN *rises, Mice (or Forest creatures) are performing a spirited dance*

### No. 11 Dance (Mice)

*At the end of the dance, Snow White is heard off R*

**Snow White** *(calling)* Hallo? Is anyone home?

*The Mice exit in a flurry. Snow White enters DR, cautiously*

I *did* knock, and the door *was* open so I ... *(She sees the room and reacts)* Oh. What a quaint little place. Who on earth can it belong to? *(She looks at the table and quickly counts)* One, two, three, four, five, six, seven. Seven bowls — seven chairs — *(she turns and sees the beds)* — and seven beds. And they're *all* only half the size they *should* be. *(She thinks)* Of course. It must be *children*. *(Puzzled)* But what are they doing all alone in the forest? Where are they now? *(Concerned)* Oh. I hope my knocking didn't frighten them. They may have run away to hide. *(Calling)* It's all right, children. I'm not going to hurt you. (*After a pause*) No answer. (*Suddenly*) Perhaps if I clean everything up, they'll realize I'm not going to harm them and come back? (*She glances around*) It could certainly *do* with having the floor swept — and the dishes washed — and a little bit of polishing wouldn't do any harm. I'll start right away.

### No. 12 Song (Snow White)

*As she sings, she gathers up the crockery, etc., from the table and takes it off. She returns and shakes and folds the cloth, picks up the broom and sweeps the floor. At the end of the song, she wipes her forehead in exhaustion*

Well, that's made a start, but there's still the dusting and polishing to do — not to mention the beds to make. And that certainly looks like a basket of dirty clothes to wash … (*She yawns*) Oh, dear. I didn't sleep a wink last night and I'm so tired. I'll just have to have a rest before I do any more. (*She yawns*) I hope they won't mind if I lie down on one of those beds. (*She leans the broom against the wall again, goes up the stairs and wearily sits on the first bed*) Oh, that's so-o-o comfortable. (*She yawns and curls up on the bed*) So — very, very, comfortable … (*Her voice trails off as she falls asleep*)

*The Lights dim slightly to indicate passing of time. Distant music is heard, then voices singing softly. The sound grows in volume*

*Suddenly the Seven Friends, led by Campion, march into the cottage* R, *their shovels, picks or sacks across their shoulders, singing lustily*

### No. 13 Song (Friends)

*They march around the cottage, tossing their impedimenta into the wings* L *as they circle the central table. Just before they sing the final note, Campion suddenly stops dead in his tracks. The others march into him and fall over backwards with yells of protest*

**Campion** (*fiercely*) Shhhhhhhhh.

*The others scramble quickly to their feet*

**Mouse-ear** (*to Campion, anxiously*) What's the matter? What is it?
**Campion** (*wide eyed and whispering*) Hasn't anybody *noticed*?
**Sorrel** (*blankly*) Noticed what?

**Campion** (*looking around cautiously*) The *room*, of course.

*They glance around, puzzled*

It's been *cleaned*.
**Others** (*in shock*) Cleaned? (*Quickly, they look around again*)
**Cloudberry** (*fearfully*) Campion's *right*. I've never seen it so tidy.
**Campion** Never mind about *that*. The question is, who *did* it?
**Butterburr** (*indignantly*) Well, don't look at *me*.
**Coltsfoot** Or me. *I* never tidy *anything*.
**Speedwell** Well, it certainly wasn't me.
**Mouse-ear** Or me.
**Sorrel** Or me.
**Cloudberry** (*puzzled*) Then who *was* it?

*All shake their heads*

**Campion** (*pulling himself up*) Gentlemen, we'd better look around.

*All fall in behind him as he tiptoes around the room peering* L *and* R *until they are back in original positions*

(*Relieved*) Well, there's nobody here now. (*Smugly*) We must have frightened them away. (*Sternly*) But next time we go out, we must remember to lock the door. (*Relaxing*) Now then, who's for dinner? (*He rubs his hands in anticipation*)
**Sorrel** (*brightly*) I'll light the fire. (*He moves towards the fireplace*)
**Mouse-ear** (*beaming*) And I'll make the soup.

*Mouse-ear exits* L

**Cloudberry** (*gloomily*) I'll get the indigestion tablets. (*He moves* DR)
**Butterburr** I'll open the windows. (*He goes to them*)

*Mouse-ear enters with a large saucepan and a basket of vegetables and goes to the table with them*

**Coltsfoot** I'll set the table.
**Speedwell** And I'll have a rest till everything's ready.

*As the others busy themselves, he goes up the stairs and sees Snow White. With a stifled cry, he turns and hurries downstairs again*

(*In a panic*) Upstairs. Upstairs. There's a monster upstairs.

*There is a big reaction from the others*

**Campion** (*wide eyed*) A monster?
**Speedwell** (*excitedly*) Covered with hair. Big white teeth. Pointed ears. Claws made of iron. Spitting fire and breathing smoke.

*The others react to the description*

And it's sleeping in *my* bed.

*They look at each other in horror*

**Campion** (*bravely*) Right, men. Everyone find a weapon. I'll show this monster he's not going to frighten *us*.

*They dash about excitedly and finally reassemble clutching various weapons: a fish slice, a feather duster, a large spoon, the sweeping brush, the saucepan, an egg whisk, a cucumber. With much hesitation, stumbling and pushing, they stealthily follow Campion up the stairs*

(*Warningly*) Shhhhhhh. (*He creeps slowly to the bed*)
**All** (*to each other*) Shhhhhhh.
**Campion** (*lifting his "weapon"*) One, two … (*He realizes what he is looking at, lowers his arm and turns to the others*) This isn't a *monster*. It's a *girl*.
**All** A girl? (*They look at each other in surprise*)
**Speedwell** (*loudly, indignantly*) Well, what's she doing in ——
**Others** (*fingers to lips, fiercely*) Shhhhhhh.
**Speedwell** (*whispering*) What's she doing in *my* bed?
**Campion** How should *I* know?
**Butterburr** Well, aren't you going to wake her?
**Campion** Certainly not. The poor child looks exhausted.
**Mouse-ear** (*protesting*) But she can't stay there all night.
**Cloudberry** (*gloomily*) I bet she can.
**Sorrel** So where are *we* going to sleep?
**Coltsfoot** There's plenty of room in the barn.
**Speedwell** (*indignantly*) With all the hens and pigs, do you mean? What about the terrible smell?
**Campion** (*easily*) Oh, don't worry about *that*. I'm sure they won't mind.
**Mouse-ear** (*gazing down at Snow White*) Isn't she beautiful?
**Butterburr** (*grumpily*) Beauty is as beauty does. (*His voice rising*) She's no right to be sleeping in *our* beds.

**Campion** (*urgently*) Keep your voice down.

**Butterburr** (*louder*) I will *not* keep my voice down. She's got no right to be here at all, and what's more I ——

*Snow White suddenly wakes and sits up, startled*

**Snow White** (*seeing them*) Oh.

**Campion** (*startled*) She's awake.

*All retreat slightly*

**Snow White** (*a little afraid*) Who are *you*?

**Campion** (*pulling himself together*) The owners of this cottage, of course. That's who *we* are.

**Mouse-ear** I'm Mouse-ear.

**Sorrel** I'm Sorrel.

**Cloudberry** I'm Cloudberry.

**Speedwell** I'm Speedwell.

**Coltsfoot** I'm Coltsfoot.

**Butterburr** I'm Butterburr.

**Campion** And I'm Campion. But who are *you*? And what are you doing in *our* cottage? (*He glares at her*)

**Snow White** Oh, please don't be cross. I'm running away from home because my stepmother wants to kill me ——

*They react in amazement*

—— but I've never been this far into the forest before, and all I've managed to do is lose myself. Yours is the first house I've seen in ages. (*Hopefully*) I was hoping you could tell me the way to Tyrolia.

**Campion** (*surprised*) Tyrolia? Why, it's over there. (*He indicates* R)

**Mouse-ear** It's through the forest ——

**Sorrel** —— over the mountains ——

**Butterburr** —— past the waterfall ——

**Cloudberry** —— along the riverside ——

**Speedwell** —— down the valley ——

**Coltsfoot** —— and over the bridge.

**Campion**
**Mouse-ear**
**Sorrel**
**Butterburr**  } (*together*) It's a long, long way.
**Cloudberry**
**Speedwell**
**Coltsfoot**

**Snow White** (*standing wearily*) Oh, dear. Then I'd better be off or I look like spending *another* night in the forest. (*Politely*) I'm so sorry to have troubled you, and thank you for your help.

*She moves past them and down the stairs*

**Campion** (*firmly*) Just a minute. Just a minute.

*He hurries down the stairs to her, followed by the others*

How do we know you're telling the truth? You haven't even told us your name. *Or* where you come from.

*The others agree*

**Snow White** (*realizing*) Oh, I'm so sorry. I'm from the royal palace. My name is Princess Millie — though everyone calls me Snow White.

*They react in astonishment*

**Mouse-ear** Snow White. But — but that means your stepmother is *Queen Maligna*.

*The others agree*

**Speedwell** And we *hate* Queen Maligna.

*The others agree*

**Coltsfoot** She's the wickedest person in the whole wide world.
**Cloudberry** And it's because of *her*, *we* have to live in hiding.

*The others agree*

**Sorrel** When *she* became Queen, she banished us because we knew who she really was — and she was scared we'd tell everyone.
**Butterburr** You see, *we* knew she was really a *witch*.
**Snow White** (*dismayed*) A witch?
**Campion** That's right. She was born in this very house, and when *she* left, *we* moved in. We'd nowhere else to go, you see.
**Snow White** (*sympathetically*) Oh, you poor things.
**Mouse-ear** (*quickly*) Oh, no. Not poor. Not *poor*. We work in our very own silver mine. Up in the mountain. (*Proudly*) We've got more silver than anyone else on earth.

**Cloudberry** (*gloomily*) Yes, but we can't sell it in case *she* finds out we're living here.

**Mouse-ear** That's why we can't hire anyone to clean the house for us.

**Speedwell** Or cook and sew.

**Butterburr** (*hopefully*) I don't suppose *you* could do it, could you?

**Sorrel** (*firmly*) Don't be silly. She's a princess. Princesses can't cook and sew.

**Snow White** (*quickly*) Oh, but I *can*. I used to help Dame Goodheart in the palace.

*All look interested*

(*Regretfully*) But I have to get to Tyrolia — to tell Prince Michael what's happened.

**Campion** (*hastily*) But — but you can't *walk* there. Not on your own. It's *very* dangerous. And we've already told you ——

**Mouse-ear** It's through the forest ——

**Sorrel** — over the mountains ——

**Butterburr** — past the waterfall ——

**Cloudberry** — along the riverside ——

**Speedwell** — down the valley ——

**Coltsfoot** — and over the bridge.

**Campion**  
**Mouse-ear**  
**Sorrel**  
**Butterburr** ⎱ (*together*) It's a long, long way.  
**Cloudberry**  
**Speedwell**  
**Coltsfoot**

**Campion** Why don't you stay with *us* for a few days? We'll send a message to Prince Michael and he can meet you here. It'll be a lot safer.

*The others agree*

**Snow White** (*doubtfully*) Well if you think that's best ——

**Mouse-ear** (*quickly*) Oh, we do.

**Others** We do.

**Snow White** (*deciding*) Then I will. And thank you.

*All look pleased*

**Speedwell** (*eagerly*) And will you clean and cook and wash for us while you're waiting?

**Others** (*anguished*) Shhhhhh. (*They gag him with their hands*)
**Snow White** (*laughing*) Of course I will.

*All react with delight*

> It'll be *my* contribution to running the house. And besides, it'll give me
> plenty of time to get to know you all better.

**No. 14** Song (Snow White and the Seven Friends)

*At the end of the song, the Lights fade rapidly to a Black-out*

SCENE 2

*A Corridor in the Palace*

*As Act I, Scene 2*

*The Fairy enters* R

**Fairy**                As with her new-found friends, Snow White
                         For now in safety dwells;
                         Court jester, Chuckles, to the queen,
                         His made-up story tells.
                         How joyfully she greets the news;
                         Her heart leaps with delight.
                         Her hated rival now lies dead
                         And all within the world is right.

*The Fairy exits*

*Queen Maligna enters* L, *followed by Chuckles who carries a small wooden
casket. She moves* R, *in a frenzy of triumphant delight*

**Queen** (*happily*) Tell me again. Tell me again. (*She swirls to face him*) Tell
me again how she *died*.
**Chuckles** (*uncomfortably*) Hiya, kids.
**Queen** (*dismissively*) Never mind those moronic mutants. I want to know
everything. *Everything*. (*Eagerly*) And don't miss out the *tiniest* detail.
(*She rubs her hands with glee*)
**Chuckles** (*flustered*) Well, you don't have to worry, Mrs Queen. You won't
ever see her again.

**Queen** (*snarling*) Of course I won't, you idiot. I already know that. I just want to hear you *say* it once more. (*She swirls around and moves* R) She's dead. She's dead. She's dead. (*She laughs harshly, then swirls around to face him*) And her heart? Did you bring me her heart?

**Chuckles** (*gulping nervously*) It's here in the box.

**Queen** (*gleefully*) Give it to me. Give it to me. (*She snatches it from him, opens the lid, peers inside and laughs with delight*) Poor deluded child. You thought your beauty could compete with mine — but where is it now? (*Triumphantly*) Gone. Gone. And I, Queen Maligna, once more am the most beautiful woman in the whole wide world.

*She laughs evilly and exits* L *with the casket*

**Chuckles** (*glaring after her*) Nasty old thing. (*To the audience, relieved*) Thank goodness she didn't spot it was only a sheep's heart in that box. (*Chortling*) She isn't half in for a shock when she finds out Snow White's still alive. (*Warningly*) But we daren't tell anybody else. Not till that Prince Michael arrives here with his army and has her locked up in jail. So remember, kids. It's our secret. Not a word to anyone. (*He grins happily*)

*Alonzo enters* L, *in tears*

**Alonzo** Oh, Chuckles, I've just heard the news. Poor Snow White. Torn to pieces in the forest and eaten by wolves. (*He dabs at his eyes with a large handkerchief*) And to think that only yesterday, she was dancing and singing the way she always did. (*Sadly*) It just shows you, doesn't it? You never know when you're going to die. (*He sobs*)

**Chuckles** My Uncle Fred did. He knew the very day — *and* the exact time.

**Alonzo** (*scornfully*) Oh, don't be ridiculous. How could he possibly know the time and day he was going to die? (*He mops at his eyes*)

**Chuckles** The judge told him. At his trial.

**Alonzo** (*upset*) Oh, I don't know *how* you can be so insensitive. Poor Snow White lying dead, everyone in the palace is mourning — and here *you* are, making silly jokes. Don't you realize? We're never going to see her again. (*He bursts into tears and turns away*)

**Chuckles** (*to the audience*) Poor Alonzo. Look how upset he is. Shall I tell him she's still alive? *He* won't tell anyone. Shall I?

*Audience response*

Yes. I will. (*To Alonzo*) Cheer up, Alonzo. There's no need to be upset. She isn't *really* dead, you know.

**Alonzo** (*turning to him*) Not dead? But the queen said.

**Chuckles** (*quickly*) Yes, I know — but it isn't true. Actually, she's run away to find that Prince Michael, and they'll *both* be back soon to give *somebody* the biggest surprise of her life.

**Alonzo** (*hopefully*) Are you sure?

**Chuckles** (*airily*) Course I am. It was *me* who took her into the forest, wasn't it? (*Remembering*) Here, but not a word to anyone else.

**Alonzo** (*hastily*) No. No Of course not. My lips are sealed. (*Happily*) Oh, I feel *so* much better now. (*He dabs his eyes*) I can't wait to tell everyone the news. (*He turns to exit*)

**Chuckles** (*yelping*) No. (*He grabs Alonzo*) I've just told you. You mustn't tell *anybody*. Otherwise it won't be a surprise.

**Alonzo** (*remembering*) Oh yes. Of course. Quite right. Mum's the word. (*He gives a little laugh*) Absolute silence.

*Alonzo exits L, beaming*

**Chuckles** (*watching him go*) Well, that's cheered *him* up. Now to find Dame Goodheart and tell her the plan's working.

*The Dame enters R, limping painfully*

**Dame** (*groaning*) Oooooh. Ohhhhhhh.

**Chuckles** I was just coming to look for *you*. (*He notices her limp*) Here, what's wrong?

**Dame** I've been trying to cook one of those new fangled sponge puddings for the queen's dinner. You know. The ones that come in a tin.

**Chuckles** (*puzzled*) Yes. But why are you limping?

**Dame** Well, I think I must have read the instructions wrong. It said "To cook this pudding, punch a hole in the lid and stand in boiling water for ten minutes." (*She winces*) Doesn't half scald your feet. And the stupid pudding's *still* not done.

**Chuckles** Yes, well, never mind that. I've given her that sheep's heart, like you said, and now she's convinced that Snow White's dead. So all that's left for us to do is wait for Prince Michael's army to arrive, and we'll be rid of her forever.

**Dame** (*brightening*) And about time, too. That's one guest I can do without at the wedding.

**Chuckles** You mean when Snow White and the prince get married.

**Dame** No, you fathead. I mean when you and me get married. (*Blissfully*) Ooooh, I can't wait to march you down the aisle.

**Chuckles** (*hastily*) But — but I can't marry you, Dame Goodheart. I'd be too nervous. I might even faint at the altar.

**Dame** Oh, don't worry about that. I'll give you artificial recreation.

**Chuckles** You mean *respiration*, don't you? Recreation's having fun.
**Dame** (*chortling*) I'm no mug.
**Chuckles** (*protesting*) But I've never been married before and I don't know
    if I'd like it.
**Dame** Of course you would. You like circuses, don't you?
**Chuckles** Oh, yes. I love circuses.
**Dame** Well then, weddings are just like three ring circuses. First comes the
    engagement ring, and next comes the wedding ring.
**Chuckles** And what comes after that?
**Dame** The suffer-ing.

**No. 15** Song (Dame and Chuckles)

*At the end of the song, the Lights fade rapidly to a Black-out*

SCENE 3

*The Queen's Private Chambers. Day*

*The backdrop depicts an arched and pillared chamber, with a view of the city
roofs, and is spectacularly decorated in gold, crimson and black. The magic
mirror is UL and hidden by velvet drapes on drawstrings. A dais is UC and atop
this is a black throne*

*When the Lights come up, Courtiers and Servants are singing and dancing
happily, led by Alonzo*

**No. 16** Song (Alonzo and Chorus)

*At the end of the song, Queen Maligna enters L*

**Queen** (*pretending to be shocked*) Such unseemly behaviour. Singing and
    dancing in *my* palace, when only a few hours ago I told you of the death of
    my poor, sweet, innocent, Snow White. (*She puts her hand to her eyes as
    though in pain*) How could you?

*All look at each other and smile secretively*

**Alonzo** (*happily*) Oh, Your Majesty, You must forgive us. But we've just
    heard the most *wonderful* news.

*All nod and smile in agreement*

**Queen** (*curious*) News?
**Alonzo** (*quickly*) But we mustn't tell *you*, Your Majesty. It's a big surprise, you see, and we don't want to spoil it for you. (*Archly*) But I *can* tell you *this* much. It's going to make you very very happy. (*He beams with delight*)
**Queen** (*with great drama*) Happy? Do you really think I can ever be happy again, when my poor Snow White lies dead in the forest? (*She turns away and pretends to sob*) Begone. All of you.

*Alonzo silently shoos them off*

*The Courtiers and Servants exit quickly with some amusement*

**Alonzo** (*kindly*) There, there, Your Majesty. Don't upset yourself. As soon as Prince Michael arrives ——
**Queen** (*startled*) Prince Michael? (*She swirls around to face him*)
**Alonzo** (*startled*) Why — er — yes, Your Majesty. He — er …
**Queen** (*snarling*) What does *he* want? Why is he coming here?
**Alonzo** (*flustered*) Well — to — er — to give you the surprise, of course.
**Queen** (*coldly*) And what exactly *is* this surprise, Lord Chamberlain? (*She takes hold of his throat; savagely*) Speak. Or I'll have your tongue torn from its roots and fed to the kitchen-hounds.
**Alonzo** (*gulping nervously*) Oh, dear. I'm sure he'd prefer to tell you himself. (*Blurting it out*) It's Snow White, Your Majesty. She isn't dead at all. She's still alive.
**Queen** (*stunned*) Alive? (*She laughs harshly*) Fool. Dolt. Idiot. (*She releases him*) Of course she's not alive. I have her pretty little heart in a casket by my bedside. (*Scornfully*) Get out of my sight before I change my mind and have you roasted on a spit for supper.

*Alonzo quickly exits* R

(*Laughing harshly*) Still alive. (*Amused*) Oh, no, my timid court chamberlain. Snow White is dead, and I, Queen Maligna, am the most beautiful woman on earth. (*She pulls on the cord to open the drapes which reveal the magic mirror*)

Mirror, mirror, on the wall,
Who is the fairest of them all?

*The Lights flicker*

*The Spirit appears in the mirror*

**Voice of the Spirit**    The claim of "Fairest in the world",
Is yours, you say, by right.
But know you this, O mighty Queen,
Much fairer still is young Snow White.

*The Queen reacts in horror*

For sheltered by her kindly friends,
In safety she will stay.
Protected from all cruel intent,
And growing lovelier ev'ry day.
**Queen** (*anguished*) It cannot be. I have her heart.
**Voice of the Spirit**    Alas, you are deceived, O Queen.
By Chuckles, were misled.
A heart of lamb is all that rests
Within the casket by your bed.
**Queen** (*seething*) So ... That miserable jester helped her escape, did he? I'll
have him hung, drawn and quartered, and his head nailed to the palace
doors by his *ears*. (*Savagely*) But first I must rid myself of Snow White.
(*She paces angrily*) But how? How? (*She sinks into thought, then suddenly
laughs delightedly*) I have it. (*To the mirror*)
Mirror, mirror, quickly tell:
Where Snow White and her friends do dwell.

*The Lights flicker*

**Voice of the Spirit**    O, mighty Queen, they hide
Within the house where you were born,
And young Prince Michael hurries there,
To claim his bride, as comes the morn.

*The face vanishes*

**Queen** (*savagely*) Over my dead body. He'll *never* marry Snow White. By
the time he reaches that cottage, she'll be deader than the (*local town*)
Councillors. (*She faces front and casts a spell*)
Claw of raven, tooth of dog.
Ear of bat and spawn of frog.

*The Lights begin to dim*

> Shriek of fear and cry of pain,
> Make me ancient, wrinkled, plain,
> Yellow toothed and grey of hair,
> Body sear, and bent with care.
> Lame of leg, and dull of eye,
> Skin like parchment, coarse and dry.
> Thick of tongue, and thin of lip,
> Flat of foot, and broad of hip.

*By this time, Maligna should be in semi-darkness*

> (*Voice rising to a climax*) O, evil spirits do your task,
> And grant the boon of thee I ask.

*There is a crash of thunder and the Lights flicker. Thick mist fills the stage*

*Spirits in flowing drapes of black and green, rush on to the stage and circle Maligna furiously, hiding her from the audience's view*

### No. 17 Dance (Spirits)

*As the dance proceeds, Maligna slips away unnoticed. Her place is taken by the "Changed" Maligna, a witch-like old crone, clutching a basket of apples. When the dance ends, the Spirits exit in a flurry*

*The Lights return to normal and the "Changed" Maligna can be seen*

**Maligna** (*cackling*) Perfect. Perfect. I'll never be recognized in this disguise. And now to deal with Snow White. (*She selects an apple, half green, half rosy*) How could she possibly resist a beautiful apple like this? (*She shows it*) Freshly picked. Crisp and sweet. (*Smiling*) And the rosy side filled with the most deadly poison on earth. One bite of *this*, and Snow White will be no more. (*She cackles happily*) To the cottage in the forest.

*She limps off L, cackling*

*A moment later, Dame and Chuckles enter uneasily, R. Chuckles is on the verge of tears*

**Chuckles** (*weepily*) Hiya, kids.
**Dame** (*annoyed*) Never mind, "Hiya, kids". If we can't persuade old Maligna it was only a joke giving her that lamb's heart, it'll be "Cheerio, kids". (*She groans*) Why on earth did you tell *Alonzo* Snow White was still

alive? Don't you know the world's fastest ways of spreading the news? Telephone, television — and tell *him*.

**Chuckles** (*unhappily*) I'm sorry. (*He wipes his eyes*)

**Dame** Oooh, you haven't got the sense you were born with. I think your nursemaid must have dropped you on your head when you were a baby.

**Chuckles** (*sniffling*) No, she didn't. We were too poor to have a nursemaid, my mother had to do it.

**Dame** (*glancing around*) Well, you may as well stop sniffling. I think we're all right for the minute. She seems to have gone out. (*She sees the mirror*) Oh. Look. The magic mirror.

**Chuckles** (*blinking*) What magic mirror?

**Dame** (*impatiently*) The one that tells the truth and never lies. (*Suddenly*) Here, I wonder if it'll tell us whether Snow White's found Prince Michael, yet? Let's give it a try.

**Chuckles** (*alarmed*) No, no. What if Queen Maligna comes back and catches us?

**Dame** Oh, never mind her. I want to find out what's happening. (*To the mirror*)

> Mirror, mirror, gleaming bright,
> Tell us where to find Snow White.

*The Lights flicker*

*The Spirit's face appears in the mirror*

**Chuckles** Blimey, it's (*well-known personality*).

**Voice of the Spirit**     A dozen leagues times seven
     In the forest deep and vast,
     Her new-found friends are hiding her
     Until all danger's past.

**Dame** (*bewildered*) New-found friends?

**Voice of the Spirit**     Within their cottage, snug and warm,
     Snow White is safe and well.
     But Queen Maligna hurries there,
     Disguised by means of magic spell.
     Such hatred fills her wicked heart,
     She's cast aside pretension:
     To kill Snow White, herself, is now
     Quite clearly her intention.

*The Spirit's face fades and vanishes*

**Dame** (*worried*) Oh, no. What are we going to do?

**Chuckles** (*bravely*) I'll tell you what we're going to do. We're going to go after her and *stop* her. She doesn't scare me, you know. (*Smugly*) You're looking at a man who doesn't know the meaning of fear. Who doesn't know the meaning of defeat, quit — or surrender.

**Dame** I think I'd better buy you a dictionary. (*Annoyed*) What are you talking about, you two-toned twerp? You're such a coward, when you go to the dentist you need an anaesthetic just to sit in the waiting-room. But you're right. (*Firmly*) We *are* going to go after her. And so is everybody else. Quick. Sound the alarm while I find out how to get there.

*Chuckles dashes off* R

*The Dame turns back to face the mirror and the Lights fade rapidly to a Black-out*


SCENE 4

*A Path through the Forest. Evening*

*The Fairy enters* R

**Fairy**              As through the woods, Maligna speeds,
                       Prince Michael hurries, too.
                       The message he has just received
                       Has proved the bad queen's tale untrue.
                       With happy heart he comes to claim
                       Snow White, his future bride;
                       That she may take her rightful place
                       Forever, at his side.

*The Fairy exits*

*Prince Michael enters* L, *a sword at his belt and carrying a roughly drawn map*

**Prince** (*referring to the map*) Well, this seems to be the right path. (*He looks off* R) That's the old oak — and I can hear the stream over there. Thank goodness Campion sent directions. I'd never be able to find my way if he hadn't. Just a few more hours and I should be at their cottage. (*Glancing around*) Poor Snow White. How frightened she must have been. All alone in the middle of this vast forest. (*Grimly*) Queen Maligna's certainly got a lot to answer for, and as soon as I've collected Snow White, we'll be heading straight for the royal palace to deal with her. (*He touches his sword hilt*) If I never do anything again in my life, I'll make quite sure *she* never hurts anyone again.

**No. 18** Song (Prince)

*At the end of the song, he exits* R

*A moment later, Dame, Chuckles and Alonzo enter uneasily* L

**Chuckles** (*to the audience*) Hiya, kids.

**Alonzo** (*concerned*) It's getting awfully dark, Dame Goodheart. Are you sure we're heading in the right direction?

**Dame** Course we are. That magic mirror said if we came this way we couldn't go wrong.

**Chuckles** Then why's everybody else gone the other way?

**Dame** (*impatiently*) Because we're going to surround her so she can't escape, fathead. Now hurry up, or we're not going to get there in time. (*She begins to move to* R)

**Chuckles** Well, I still think we should have followed her with a bloodhound. They aren't half good at tracking people.

**Alonzo** (*interested*) Really?

**Chuckles** Yes. All they have to do is sniff at something the missing person wore, and they can follow 'em for miles.

**Alonzo** (*impressed*) You mean, it could follow the scent of Queen Maligna's faint perfume, for instance?

**Dame** (*scornfully*) Course it couldn't. It's not called faint perfume for nothing, you know. One sniff of that stuff, and the *dog*'d faint. Anyway, I'm not having any dogs near me. I don't trust 'em. I was standing on (*local street*) corner last week, waiting to cross the road, and this massive great dog came up to me and lifted his back leg like this ... (*She demonstrates*) I've never moved so fast in my life. I thought it was going to kick me.

**Chuckles** (*scornfully*) Give over. Anyway, we'd have been a lot safer if we'd have had a dog with us. It could have frightened off anything scarey.

**Alonzo** (*nervously*) Scarey?

**Chuckles** Well, it's a bit creepy in these woods, isn't it? They could be haunted, for all we know.

**Dame** (*scornfully*) Could be haunted. (*Annoyed*) How could they be haunted, when there's no such thing as ghosts?

**Chuckles** Oh, yes, there are. My Uncle Bert got chased by one once. It followed him round the palace dungeons, up ten flights of stairs, down five miles of corridors, and finally managed to catch him by the ramparts. (*He winces*) Ooooh. It didn't half make his eyes water.

**Dame** (*uncertainly*) Well, even if there *are* any ghosts, there's nothing to be scared of. We could frighten 'em away, couldn't we?

**Alonzo** (*doubtfully*) Could we?

**Dame** (*firmly*) Course we could. Everybody knows ghosts don't like singing, so all we have to do is sing a little song, and they'd be off like a rocket.

**Chuckles** Well, why don't we try it? Just to make sure nothing nasty and horrible creeps up on us without us noticing.

**Alonzo** Good idea. And perhaps all the girls and boys in the audience could shout out and warn us if something *does* come along? (*To the audience*) Would you do that, girls and boys? Would you?

*Audience response*

**Chuckles** Well, that's all right then. Now what are we going to sing?

**Alonzo** (*coyly*) "Has Anybody Seen My Tiddler"?

**Dame** (*after a reaction*) I don't think we want to know the answer to that one. Let's sing something we *all* know.

*They decide on a song and begin to sing*

**No. 19** Song (Dame, Chuckles and Alonzo)

*The Ghost enters* L, *crosses* R *quickly and exits*

*Audience reaction. All stop singing*

**Chuckles** (*to the audience*) What's the matter? What is it?

*Audience response*

**Alonzo** (*scared*) A ghost. They've seen a ghost.

**Dame** Well, *I* didn't see anything. (*To Chuckles*) Did you?

**Chuckles** Not a sausage. But if they say they've seen one, we'd better have a look round, just to make sure.

*With great caution, they tip-toe round in a circle*

*The Ghost enters* R, *tags on end of line and exits* L

*The others reach their original position*

**Dame** (*disgustedly*) There's nothing there at all. They're having us on.

**Alonzo** (*to the audience*) Naughty children. Frightening us like that.
**Chuckles** No, wait. Wait. They weren't having us on. They were having a
practice.
**Dame** (*realizing*) Oh, a practice. Well, that's all right then. We know we're
safe now. Let's carry on singing.

*They begin singing again*

*The Ghost enters* L, *and exits* R

*Ad-lib and repeat routine as before but in opposite direction. After Ad-libs
with audience, they begin singing again*

*The Ghost enters* L, *moves to Alonzo and taps him on the shoulder. Alonzo
looks round, shrieks and hurries off* L, *followed by the Ghost*

*After a moment, the others realize he is gone and stop singing*

**Chuckles** (*surprised*) Here. Where's *he* gone? (*To the audience*) Did you see
where he went? (*He ad libs with the audience*)
**Dame** Well, never mind about *him*. It's much cosier being just the *two* of us.
More *romantic*, wouldn't you say? (*She tweaks her lips at him*)
**Chuckles** (*hastily*) Let's carry on singing.

*They begin singing again*

*The Ghost enters* L, *crosses to Chuckles and taps him on the shoulder.
Chuckles turns, sees it, screams and exits* L, *followed by the Ghost*

*After a moment, the Dame notices he is missing and stops singing*

**Dame** (*blankly*) Chuckles? Chuckles? (*Worried*) Ooh, I say — *he*'s gone as
well. (*To the audience*) It wasn't a ghost, was it?

*Audience response*

(*Worried*) Oh, dear. Now I'll have to sing on my own. (*Airily*) Mind you,
I'm very musical. I was born with a drum in each ear.

*She begins singing again*

*The Ghost enters* L, *crosses to the Dame and taps her on the shoulder*

*The Dame looks round*

*The Ghost shrieks with fright and exits followed by Dame*

*The Lights fade rapidly to a Black-out*

SCENE 5

*Outside the Cottage. Day*

*A forest backdrop. A rostrum runs L to R, and there are grassy steps L leading down to the main acting area. The cottage is R of the steps, and has a practical door. By the side of this is a small wooden pail. A groundrow of shrubbery is to L of the cottage, hiding the rostrum. In front of the shrubbery is a brightly coloured handcart, its handles to the audience. Trees mask exits R and L*

*The Lights come up on the Seven Friends entering in a line from the cottage, singing happily. Their working tools over their shoulders, they march round the stage in a large circle. They are followed by Snow White, who carries seven small packages of wrapped sandwiches. She stands by the cottage door and hands over a package to each as he passes her. After the last sandwich has been taken, she joins them in their dance*

**No. 20** Song  (The Seven Friends and Snow White)

*At the end of the song, Snow White should be R and the others L*

**Snow White**  Now don't forget. There'll be freshly baked bread and beef stew for dinner, so don't be late home.

**Campion**  Don't worry, Snow White. Beef stew's our very favourite dinner.

**Sorrel**  Beef stew and *dumplings*. (*Anxiously*) There *will* be dumplings, won't there?

**Snow White**  (*laughing*) Of course there will.

**Mouse-Ear**  (*eagerly*) And honey pancakes?

**Butterburr**  And blackberry pie?

**Snow White**  (*amused*) I think I can manage those.

**Cloudberry**  (*dispiritedly*) But no cherry cakes.

**Snow White**  Well, perhaps a *few*.

*Cloudberry brightens*

**Coltsfoot**  (*hopefully*) And a chocolate one?

**Snow White** (*smiling*) And a chocolate one.

**Speedwell** (*gloomily*) Hmph. And I bet it's *my* turn to do the washing up.

**Snow White** (*laughing*) Don't worry, Speedwell. I'll have everything washed up before you arrive. All *you'll* have to do is eat. (*Briskly*) Now off you go or you won't have started work before it's time to come home again.

**Campion** (*to the others*) Snow White's right. Come along, men. Off to the silver mine.

**Mouse-Ear** Cheerio, Snow White. We'll be back before nightfall. And remember what we told you. Don't let anyone inside until *we* arrive home.

**Sorrel** Yes. Queen Maligna might know you're still alive and be out looking for you.

*The others agree*

**Snow White** But she'd never find me *here*. It's a long long way from the palace.

**Coltsfoot** Better safe than sorry. You musn't forget she's really a witch, and witches can find out *anything*.

*The others agree*

**Speedwell** And *we* want you to be safe till Prince Michael arrives.

**Snow White** (*sighing*) If only we knew he'd got the message you sent.

**Cloudberry** Of course he did. Our friend the blackbird took it to the palace himself and promised to leave it on the prince's pillow. He'll be halfway here by now.

**Snow White** Oh, I *do* hope so.

**Butterburr** (*impatiently*) Yes. And if we don't get to work soon, we'll still be here when he arrives.

**Sorrel** Butterburr's right. Let's be off.

**Campion** (*briskly*) Right, then. Shoulder tools, men.

*The friends shoulder their tools*

Cheerio, Snow White.

**Others** Bye.

*They sing a reprise of the scene's opening song, and as they do so, once again execute a large circle before ascending the steps and marching along the rostrum*

*They exit behind the cottage*

*Snow White waves goodbye to them. Their voices fade away in the distance*

**Snow White**  And now to start *my* work. I'd better heat some water so I can wash up the breakfast dishes. (*She turns and picks up the wooden pail*)

**Maligna**  (*off* L, *in a cracked voice*) Apples for sale. Apples for sale.

**Snow White**  (*turning, surprised*) An apple seller? In the middle of the forest?

*The disguised Maligna enters* L, *with her apple basket*

**Maligna**  (*limping* C) Good-morning, my dear. Lovely apples for sale. (*She indicates the basket*) Would you like to buy some?

**Snow White**  (*happily*) Why, yes. (*Remembering*) I mean — no. (*Quickly*) I mean — yes, I *would* like to buy some — but — to tell you the truth — I haven't any money.

**Maligna**  Oh, dear. (*Smiling*) Then I'll tell you what I'll do. Let me come inside your pretty cottage and sit by the fire, and I'll give you an apple for nothing.

**Snow White**  Why, thank you. (*She remembers*) But I'm afraid I can't invite you in. It's not my cottage, you see, and I've been told not to let anyone in until the owners came home again.

**Maligna**  (*wistfully*) Not even a poor old apple seller?

**Snow White**  (*regretfully*) I'm sorry.

**Maligna**  (*smiling*) Not to worry. The sun's warm enough to ease my aching bones. And you shall have your apple, anyway. (*She selects an apple from her basket*) Here we are, ripe and juicy — just perfect for your dainty teeth and pretty lips. (*She holds out the apple*)

**Snow White**  (*uncertainly*) You're very kind — but — I don't think I should.

**Maligna**  (*chuckling*) Nonsense, child. There's not an apple in the world as sweet as this. Just one little bite, and I promise you'll be in heaven. (*She turns her head aside and cackles*)

**Snow White**  Well — it *does* look delicious. (*She decides*) All right. I'll try it. (*She puts down the pail and holds out her hand*)

**Maligna**  (*giving her the apple*) There we are, my dear. Try the rosy side first.

**Snow White**  Thank you. (*She bites the rosy side*) Oh. It tastes so — Ohhhhhhh.

*She falls to the ground and lies still. Maligna shrieks with laughter*

**Maligna**  So dies Snow White, and I, Queen Maligna, at last am fairest of them all.

*She shrieks with laughter again and exits quickly* L

*The Fairy enters* R

**Fairy**  Alas, upon the leafy ground, Princess Snow White lay dead,
Whilst thoughts of jubilation filled vile Queen Maligna's head.

*The Lights begin to fade*

And as the hours passed slowly by, as ever is the way,
The golden sun began to sink, and night replaced the day.
Then from the distant mountain peak where sighing winds made moan,
The weary friends, on tired feet, at last returned to home.

*The Fairy exits* R. *As she does so, the Friends are heard singing wearily a reprise of their exit song. They enter along the rostrum* R, *led by Campion, descend the steps and see Snow White. The singing stops at once, they drop their tools and hurry to her*

**Friends**  (*anxiously*) Snow White. Snow White.
**Campion**  (*kneeling beside her*) She's dead.

*They react in disbelief*

**Mouse-Ear**  But what happened?
**Sorrel**  (*pointing*) Look. An apple in her hand. And there's one bite missing.
**Butterburr**  (*horrified*) It must have been a poisoned apple.
**Cloudberry**  You mean — a French Golden Delicious?

*They begin to cry*

**Coltsfoot**  But who could have given it to her?
**Speedwell**  (*sniffling*) That rotten old Queen Maligna — that's who. She must have followed her here after all. (*He sobs*)
**Campion**  (*sadly*) What shall we tell Prince Michael? This is all our fault. We should never have left her alone.
**Cloudberry**  (*upset*) Poor Snow White. All we can do *now* is dig her a grave.
**Butterburr**  (*mopping at his eyes*) And first thing tomorrow morning, I'll pick the most beautiful flowers in the forest to put on her coffin.
**Coltsfoot**  (*sniffling*) I can't believe we'll never see her again.
**Speedwell**  *And* we'll have to do our own housework. (*He sobs*)

*The others all glare at him*

**Sorrel** (*wistfully*) If you didn't know she was dead, you'd think she was sleeping, wouldn't you? (*He wipes his tears*)

**Mouse-Ear** (*sighing*) She's so beautiful. It's a shame we've got to cover her up.

*The others nod sadly*

**Campion** (*suddenly*) But we don't. We *don't* have to cover her up. We'll put her in a glass coffin over there — (*he indicates handcart*) — then we can see her every day and never forget her.

*The others agree with excitement and they crowd around Snow White. The Lights fade to a Black-out. Running tabs are brought across to hide the scene*

*The Fairy enters* DR *in a white spot*

**Fairy**                 With heavy hearts, the little men
                          Laid poor Snow White to rest
                          Inside a casket made of glass
                          And placed wild flowers at her breast.
                          All through the weary night they stood,
                          And prayers they softly spake.
                          They gazed upon her silent form,
                          And sobbed as though their hearts would break.
                          But by and by came morning,
                          And, as brighter grew the day,
                          Her loving friends arrived in haste,
                          To find her as in state she lay.

*She brandishes her wand and exits*

*The Lights come up to full again. The running tabs open to reveal Snow White in the glass casket atop the handcart. She holds a posy of wild flowers to her chest. The Friends surround the cart, kneeling, their heads bowed*

**Prince** (*off,* UR) Snow White. Snow White.

*He hurries on along the rostrum, and stops* C, *gazing in dismay at the glass casket. As he does so, Dame, Chuckles, and Alonzo quickly enter* DL. *They are followed by the Chorus who enter* L *and* R. *All look at the casket in horror*

What happened? (*He hurries to the casket*)

**Campion** (*rising sadly*) She's been poisoned by Queen Maligna.

*The Friends rise sadly*

**Chuckles** (*in disbelief*) Oh, no.
**Dame** (*distraught*) My little princess. (*She sobs*)

*Chuckles comforts her. The Chorus huddle together*

**Alonzo** (*tearfully*) It's all my fault. I should never have told her Snow White was still alive. (*He mops at his eyes*)
**Prince** (*gazing at the casket, despairingly*) And to think that tomorrow would have been our wedding day.
**Chuckles** (*sniffling*) Well, what are we going to do now? We can't just leave her here.
**Prince** (*sadly*) I suppose you're right. We'll take her to Tyrolia ... (*Grimly*) and then I'm coming straight back to Sylvania to settle with Queen Maligna, once and for all. (*He moves* c)
**Mouse-Ear** (*protesting*) But — we want Snow White to stay with *us*.
**Sorrel** Yes. She was *our* friend.
**Butterburr** *We* were the ones who looked after her.
**Coltsfoot** We don't *want* you to take her away.
**Cloudberry** No. She belongs to *us*.
**Speedwell** She's ours. All ours.
**Campion** (*fiercely*) You shan't have her. (*He stands in front of the casket, arms outstretched*)
**Prince** (*stepping forward*) But she can't stay here in the *forest*.
**Campion** She can. She can. (*He steps back and bumps into the cart*) Owwww.

*Everyone gasps as Snow White coughs and sits up*

**Prince** (*amazed*) Snow White. You're alive. But how?
**Snow White** (*dazedly*) Where am I?
**Mouse-Ear** (*excitedly*) The piece of apple. She hadn't swallowed it. It fell out of her mouth when you bumped against the cart.

*They quickly help Snow White to her feet amid great excitement. As the Prince and Snow White embrace, the others congratulate them and dance around delightedly*

*At the height of the excitement, Maligna, no longer in disguise, appears on the rostrum behind them in a towering rage*

**Maligna** So.

*Everyone turns and sees her*

Once more my will is thwarted. But with the aid of my magic sword I'll carve you all into tiny pieces. (*She produces a glittering sword*)

*Everyone gasps and steps back*

**Prince**  Not so fast, Maligna. This time you have *me* to reckon with. (*He draws his sword*)
**Maligna** (*snarling*) You puny poppinjay. Your sword is no match for mine.

*She descends the steps, sword at the ready*

Prepare to die. (*She lunges at him*)

*A fierce fight ensues between the Prince and Maligna. The others react. At first, the Queen appears to be winning, but suddenly the Prince drives his sword into her. With an anguished cry, she drops her sword, staggers UL, and falls to the ground*

**Prince** (*triumphantly*) So dies Maligna, and Snow White becomes Queen of Sylvania.

*All cheer and kneel to her*

**Snow White** (*fondly*) My dearest friends. I don't know how to thank you for everything you've done. But one thing I promise. Everyone in Sylvania will be invited to my wedding with Prince Michael — and Campion, Mouse-ear, Sorrel, Cloudberry, Butterburr, Coltsfoot and Speedwell will be our special guests of honour.

*Everyone is delighted*

**Prince** (*rising*) And from that moment on, the only crime in the kingdom will be *not* to be happy. So back to the palace without delay — and we'll meet again on our wedding day.

*All cheer*

### No. 21 Song  (Company)

*At the end of the song, the Lights fade rapidly to a Black-out*

## Scene 6

*A Corridor in the Palace*

*Chuckles enters*

**Chuckles** Hiya, kids.

*Audience response*

Well, it's all over now. Queen Maligna's dead, Snow White and the prince
are getting married, the Seven Friends have given 'em buckets of diamonds
for a wedding present, and I'm just on my way to the Jobcentre to see if I
can hire some singers for the choir. (*He thinks*) Hang about, though. I don't
need to hire singers, do I? Course not. I bet you lot can sing as well as
anybody. And it'll give you a chance to come to the wedding, won't it?
Course it will. So I'll see who's got the best voices, and then we'll be off
to the wedding.

*He ad libs into the song sheet. Continue as required*

**No. 22** Song (Song Sheet)

*At the end of the song, Chuckles exits*

*The Lights fade rapidly to a Black-out*

## Scene 7

*The Great Ballroom and Finale*

*A spectacular ballroom with rostra and steps,* UC

*When the Lights come up, Dancers are dancing a lively routine*

**No. 23** Dance

*At the end of the routine, all exit*

*As they do so, Juniors enter on rostra, descending the steps to begin the
walk down as follows:*

Juniors
Dancers
Chorus
Voice of the Spirit (*carrying mirror*)
Fairy
Alonzo
The Seven Friends
Queen Maligna
Dame Goodheart
Chuckles
Snow White and Prince Michael

**Fairy**  Our pantomime is over, and wrong is put to right.
Now all that's left to do for us is bid you all "Good-night".
We trust we've entertained you all with song and joyful laughter,
And hope that just like us, you'll live in happiness for ever after.

*Everyone sings a reprise of the Finale song*

**No. 23a** Song

CURTAIN

# FURNITURE AND PROPERTY LIST

## ACT I

### PROLOGUE

*On stage*:    Nil

*Personal*:    **Fairy**: wand

### SCENE 1

*On stage*:    Half-timbered houses and shops cut-outs

*Off stage*:    Shopping bag containing get-well card (**Dame**)
Large mirror wrapped in paper (**Alonzo**)
String of brightly coloured balloons (**Chuckles**)
Gift-wrapped box (**Prince Michael**)

*Personal*:    **Alonzo**: large calendar

### SCENE 2

*On stage*:    Nil

### SCENE 3

*On stage*:    Small dais. *On it*: ornate throne

*Personal*:    **Alonzo**: rod of office

### SCENE 4

*On stage*:    Nil

### SCENE 5

*On stage*:    Tree flats
Grassy mound

*Off stage*:    Picnic basket (**Dame**)
Picnic baskets, hampers (**Citizens**)
Small posy of wild flowers (**Snow White**)

*Personal*:    **Chuckles**: dagger in belt, envelope containing letter

ACT II

Scene 1

*On stage*:   Fireplace
              Roughly carved wooden table. *On it*: dirty cloth, 7 small bowls with
                 wooden spoons, 7 beakers, cracked milk jug, large ceramic teapot,
                 open butter dish, buttery knife, wooden bread board, half a cottage
                 loaf, bread knife
              7 rickety wooden chairs
              Carved broom with straw head
              Basket. *In it*: dirty washing
              Feather duster
              Large spoon
              Egg whisk
              7 beds. *On each*: pillow, faded patchwork quilt

*Off stage*:  Shovels, picks, sacks (**Friends**)
              Large saucepan, basket of vegetables including cucumber (**Mouse-
                 ear**)

Scene 2

*On stage*:   Nil

*Off stage*:  Small wooden casket (**Chuckles**)

*Personal*:   **Alonzo**: large handkerchief

Scene 3

*On stage*:   Magic mirror behind velvet drapes on drawstring
              Dais. *On it*: black throne

*Off stage*:  Basket of apples (**Maligna**)

Scene 4

*On stage*:   Nil

*Off stage*:  Map (**Prince Michael**)

*Personal*:   **Prince Michael**: sword

Scene 5

*On stage*:   Cottage cut-out with practical door. *Beside it*: small wooden pail
              Rostrum with shrubbery groundrow

Grassy steps
Handcart
Tree cut-outs

*Off stage*: 7 small packets of sandwiches (**Snow White**)

DURING BLACK-OUT ON PAGE 52

*Set*: Glass casket on top of handcart
Posy of flowers for **Snow White**

*Off stage*: Glittering sword (**Maligna**)

SCENE 6

*On stage*: Nil

SCENE 7

*On stage*: Rostra with steps

# LIGHTING PLOT

Property fittings required: nil

Various interior and exterior settings

ACT I, Prologue

*To open*: Black-out

| | | |
|---|---|---|
| *Cue* 1 | The **Fairy** enters | (Page 1) |
| | *Follow spot on* **Fairy** | |


ACT I, Scene 1

*To open*: Bright sunshine

| | | |
|---|---|---|
| *Cue* 2 | The **Dame** preens and simpers | (Page 5) |
| | *Lighting flickers* | |
| *Cue* 3 | **Queen**: "... fairest in this land?" | (Page 6) |
| | *Lighting flickers* | |
| *Cue* 4 | **Queen**: "You lie." | (Page 6) |
| | *Lighting flickers* | |
| *Cue* 5 | **Snow White** and the **Prince** move off together | (Page 11) |
| | *Fade to black-out* | |


ACT I, Scene 2

*To open*: General interior lighting downstage

| | | |
|---|---|---|
| *Cue* 6 | The **Queen** exits laughing | (Page 15) |
| | *Fade to black-out* | |


ACT I, Scene 3

*To open*: Full general lighting

# Lighting Plot

*Cue* 7     At the end of song (no. 6)     (Page 19)
         *Quick fade to black-out*

ACT I, Scene 4

*To open*: General interior lighting downstage

*Cue* 8     **Queen**: "... fairest of them all?"     (Page 19)
         *Lighting flickers*

*Cue* 9     The **Queen** exits L     (Page 21)
         *Fade to black-out*

ACT I, Scene 5

*To open*: Dappled morning effect

*Cue* 10     The **Fairy** enters     (Page 22)
         *White follow spot on* **Fairy**

*Cue* 11     The **Dame** and **Chuckles** exit DL     (Page 28)
         *Begin slow dim; continue*

*Cue* 12     **Fairy**: "Throughout the moonlit night."     (Page 28)
         *Slowly change to moonlight effect*

ACT II, Scene 1

*To open*: Full general lighting

*Cue* 13     **Snow White** falls asleep     (Page 30)
         *Dim lighting slightly*

*Cue* 14     At the end of song (no. 14)     (Page 36)
         *Quick fade to black-out*

ACT II, Scene 2

*To open*: General interior lighting downstage

*Cue* 15     At the end of song (no. 15)     (Page 39)
         *Quick fade to black-out*

ACT II, Scene 3

*To open*:  Full general lighting

| | | |
|---|---|---|
| *Cue* 16 | **Queen**: "... fairest of them all?"<br>*Lighting flickers* | (Page 40) |
| *Cue* 17 | **Queen**: "... her friends do dwell."<br>*Lighting flickers* | (Page 41) |
| *Cue* 18 | **Queen**: "... spawn of frog."<br>*Lighting begins to dim; continue* | (Page 41) |
| *Cue* 19 | **Queen**: "... of thee I ask."<br>*Lighting flickers* | (Page 42) |
| *Cue* 20 | **Dame**: "... to find Snow White."<br>*Lighting flickers* | (Page 43) |
| *Cue* 21 | The **Dame** turns to face the mirror<br>*Quick fade to black-out* | (Page 44) |

ACT II, Scene 4

*To open*:  Dim lighting downstage

| | | |
|---|---|---|
| *Cue* 22 | The **Ghost** and **Dame** exit<br>*Quick fade to black-out* | (Page 48) |
| *Cue* 23 | **Fairy**: "... filled vile Queen Maligna's head."<br>*Start slow fade* | (Page 51) |
| *Cue* 24 | They crowd around **Snow White**<br>*Fade to black-out* | (Page 52) |
| *Cue* 25 | The **Fairy** enters<br>*White follow spot on* **Fairy** | (Page 52) |
| *Cue* 26 | The **Fairy** exits<br>*Bring up full general lighting* | (Page 52) |
| *Cue* 27 | At the end of song (no. 22)<br>*Quick fade to black-out* | (Page 55) |

ACT II, SCENE 6

*To open*:  General interior lighting downstage

*Cue* 28       At the end of song (no. 22)                          (Page 55)
               *Quick fade to black-out*


ACT II, SCENE 7

*To open*:  Full general lighting

No cues

# EFFECTS PLOT

## ACT I

*Cue* 1     **Chuckles**: "Well ..."                           (Page 17)
                  *Fanfare*

*Cue* 2     **Fairy**: "Throughout the moonlit night."      (Page 28)
                  *Dry ice*

## ACT II

*Cue* 3     **Queen**: "... of thee I ask."                    (Page 42)
                  *Crash of thunder, dry ice*